PRAISE FOR *EMBRACING OUR ROOTS*

"Paul J. Palma explores ethno history as an Italian American Pentecostal who has learned to successfully navigate divergent worlds. He displays affection for his own heritage, showing how it has contributed immeasurably to his own life. An inspiring and provocative read firmly grounded in both cultural diversity and church history, this book speaks to the broad needs of a diverse reading audience, and will help others to appreciate their own unique ethnic and spiritual heritage."

—Joseph J. Saggio, executive vice president, Southwestern Assemblies of God University: American Indian College

"In a rich biographical and self-exploratory excursion, Paul Palma dismantles prevailing understandings of Italian American ethnoracial identity, religious tradition, and history in the United States. Reflecting on his Italian ancestry, he exposes the social discrimination and marginalization these people faced upon their arrival in the United States. He uncovers that not all Italians were Catholic. Among them, there emerged a strong contingent of Pentecostals, who formed what would become, today, the International Fellowship of Christian Assemblies. In the end, he brings it all together under the rubric of being made in the image of God. This affirmation rejects destructive racist attitudes that can be countered through learning to value other humans as God's creatures."

—Néstor Medina, assistant professor, Emmanuel College of Victoria University in the University of Toronto

"Paul Palma takes us on a journey. He shares a glimpse into his family history, but more than that, draws readers into serious reflection about their own lives. Specifically, he urges readers to consider the importance of their relationships, with family members and with God, as this dimension of life, more than any other, contributes to the shaping of who we are. His words may be just the reset some people need."

—John P. Lathrop, author of *Answer the Prayer of Jesus: A Call for Biblical Unity*

"Since the beginning of history, people have been on the move for various reasons. Paul describes the beauty and challenges of diversity in the American cultural context by making a theistic journey to his Italian roots. Through excellent academic research and constructive transparency about his personal life, he persuasively writes that it is vital to comprehend one's origin, the cultural and religious influences that build personality, to understand who you are clearly. The book contains appealing and helpful insights to those who struggle to adjust to a foreign culture and personal health issues."

—Alex Mekonnen, associate professor, Regent University

Embracing Our Roots

Embracing Our Roots

Rediscovering the Value of Faith, Family, and Tradition

PAUL J. PALMA

EMBRACING OUR ROOTS
Rediscovering the Value of Faith, Family, and Tradition

Copyright © 2021 Paul J. Palma. All rights reserved. Except for brief quotations in critical publications or reviews, no part of this book may be reproduced in any manner without prior written permission from the publisher. Write: Permissions, Wipf and Stock Publishers, 199 W. 8th Ave., Suite 3, Eugene, OR 97401.

Scripture quotations marked (NIV) are taken from the Holy Bible, New International Version®, NIV®. Copyright © 1973, 1978, 1984, 2011 by Biblica, Inc.® Used by permission of Zondervan. All rights reserved worldwide. www.zondervan.com The "NIV" and "New International Version" are trademarks registered in the United States Patent and Trademark Office by Biblica, Inc.®

Scripture quotations marked (NLT) are taken from the Holy Bible, New Living Translation, copyright ©1996, 2004, 2015 by Tyndale House Foundation. Used by permission of Tyndale House Publishers, a Division of Tyndale House Ministries, Carol Stream, Illinois 60188. All rights reserved.

Scripture quotations marked (NRSV) are from the New Revised Standard Version Bible, copyright © 1989 National Council of the Churches of Christ in the United States of America. Used by permission. All rights reserved worldwide.

Wipf & Stock
An Imprint of Wipf and Stock Publishers
199 W. 8th Ave., Suite 3
Eugene, OR 97401

www.wipfandstock.com

PAPERBACK ISBN: 978-1-7252-9314-4
HARDCOVER ISBN: 978-1-7252-9315-1
EBOOK ISBN: 978-1-7252-9316-8

03/22/21

To my parents, Tim and Joy Palma. Thank you for your exemplary walk of faith, godly service, and many years of loving guidance.

Contents

Illustrations	xi
Acknowledgments	xiii
Prologue	xv
Introduction	1

PART I: VALUING OUR HERITAGE

1	Sunday Dinner: Making an Ethno-Faith Tradition	11
2	I May Not Look It, but I'm "FBI": Towards a Healthy Ethnocentrism	20
3	Enjoying an Afternoon Siesta	27
4	Where We Come From, and What We're Made Of	33

PART II: FOSTERING OUR IDENTITY

5	How We Got Here: Rediscovering Our Migrant Identity	43
6	Not Just Another Rags to Riches Story: Ethnic Identity and Social Class	59
7	Forays into the Problem of Racial Identity	65
8	On Being a Religious Italian American, but Not a Good Catholic	78
9	What Makes Me Pentecostal	90

PART III: LIVING OUT OUR VALUES

10	*La famiglia*	101
11	Navigating Gender in Home and Church	111
12	Towards a Holistic Approach to Well-Being	117
13	Finding Wholeness	126
	Epilogue	133

Appendix A: How to Build Your Family History	139
Appendix B: My Family Tree	145
Bibliography	149
Subject Index	161
Scripture Index	167

Illustrations

PLATES

5.1	Michele and Catherina Palma	55
5.2	Massimiliano and Maria Tosetto	56
5.3	Angelo and Carmela Rubbo	57
5.4	Vincenzo and Elisabetta Stigliano	58

CHARTS

Appendix B.1 Paternal Ancestry	146
Appendix B.2 Maternal Ancestry	147

Acknowledgments

Undertaking a book of this kind is a journey done in collaboration. Credit is owed to many along the way who generously contributed to the final shape of this work.

First of all, I am indebted to several colleagues who graciously gave of their time to read and comment on portions of the manuscript: Joseph Saggio, Néstor Medina, Alemayehu Mekonnen, John Lathrop, Diane Chandler, and Dominick Hankle. I am also thankful to the Regent University library staff, who has been more than accommodating to my numerous requests throughout the writing process. Special thanks are due to Patty Hughson and her exceptional interlibrary loan team.

The enthusiastic staff at Wipf and Stock have been a constant resource throughout this project. I owe a particular debt of gratitude to Matthew Wimer, Savanah N. Landerholm, and George Callihan, each of whom has been a reliable hands-on partner at the various writing and production stages.

In many respects, this book is a deep-seated tribute to the memory of my ancestors who, in life, modeled exemplarity and, in death, bequeathed a legacy. Foremost, I want to commemorate the heritage of my grandparents, Alfred and Esther Palma and Joseph and Theresa Rubbo, my step-grandmother, Santa Rubbo, and my great-Aunt, Esther Stigliano.

Over the course of this work, I have had the opportunity to reconnect with or foment brand new ties with my extended family. I am immensely grateful to those who gave of their time to converse with or email me about our shared heritage, notably my great-Aunt Febe Palma; cousins Vincent Stigliano, Douglas Davis, Roger Telschow, Kristin Hemmings, Maggie Rubbo-Liguori; and Linda BonGiovanni Abraham.

Thanks are due to my brother David for sharing notes from his family-tree work, and to my sister, Laura Joy, for her insightful review of portions of the manuscript. I am most appreciative of my mom, Joy, for the droves of inherited materials (photos, articles, bios, and correspondences) that have helped me plumb the rich experiences of my forebears. Our many conversations over the last few years opened the door to countless new avenues of research.

Finally, I am sincerely grateful to my wife, Gabrielle. Thank you for your review of the manuscript and the many endearing conversations from the very beginning of this project. Without your constant guidance and encouragement, this book would not have been possible.

Prologue

THE RECENT LOSS OF my paternal grandmother, Esther Palma, and maternal great-Aunt, Esther Stigliano, catalyzed a new resolve to revisit and write on my roots. Both were nonagenarians and represented in life a window into the world and ways of a cherished yet overlooked generation. This book harkens to their legacy, and that of the prior generation who, as Italian immigrants, braved the New World on behalf of subsequent kin.

This work was motivated by a desire to revisit my family heritage. As such, it is filled with personal anecdotes about my growing-up years and experiences today as a husband and father of three. In writing about my heritage, I found that reconnecting with my roots enriched my life in more ways than one, inspiring me to devise the book in a way that would invite others to join along on what has been a *journey of rediscovery*. We each are confronted with specific contrasts between our family life (how we were raised and build our homes today) and contemporary culture. Arriving at this precipice, at the intersection of family and culture, offers an opportunity for reflection.

I am a six-foot-three, light-skinned, light-haired, light-eyed, third-generation Pentecostal Italian American. While I do not look or worship like the average Italian, I'm an "FBI"—a full-blooded Italian (with proof from Ancestry DNA!). I know firsthand how challenging it can be to live between cultures. Growing up in a family of immigrants, I became keenly familiar with the outside world's pressure to assimilate. I was constantly forced to reconcile my "Italianness" with my "Americanness." Moreover, even among my "own" people, fellow Italian Americans, I was faced with the disparity of our family's faith commitment. In a society where most Italian Americans are Catholics, I was a Pentecostal. My forebears once faced the genuine threat of excommunication from the "Mother Church." I had to learn to accept my "Pentecostalness" despite the Catholic identity of the typical Italian.

I am an American. But not just an American. I am an Italian American. My ancestry traces to Italy, and not just some of my lineage, but each branch of my family tree. Since the late nineteenth century, my forebears have lived in the United States, entering the country as part of the Great Migration of Italian peasants. Since then, America has left an indelible imprint on how we think, feel, and live. At the same time, we have never shrunken from our Italianness, very intentionally preserving aspects of our Italian identity.

Concerning faith commitment, I consider myself a Pentecostal. But I am not just a Pentecostal. During my thirty-nine years on earth, I have attended a Pentecostal church for three or four of them. My parents grew up as pastor's kids in Pentecostal congregations, with my grandparents devoting their entire lives to church ministry. Having inherited this background, I have never been able to escape my Pentecostalness. On the other hand, I currently belong to the United Methodist Church. When asked what denomination I am a member of, the simple answer is "Methodist." Nevertheless, when asked to describe my religious leanings, I usually include "Pentecostal" in the tag. I have a soft spot for Pentecostals. In the Western world, Pentecostals are often given the cold shoulder for their purported emotionalism and "babbling" (speaking in tongues). My forebears' years in the Pentecostal ministry have inspired me to find common ground between Pentecostals and other walks of faith.

This book is an attempt to reach beyond the labels, presuppositions, and stereotypes that define who we are. I propose that the path forward rests in building for us a broader context. We are each part of a grander narrative, not chiefly defined by our outlying appearance or circumstances, but by the people we come from. In looking to our ancestry, no matter how vibrant or bleak we think it is, we expand the referent, so to speak, allowing us to move past surface matters to the relational dimension of who we are. When we interpret ethnic or religious monikers in light of our family history, we prove the label's sincerity. Indeed, I may be "Italian," "American," "Pentecostal," and "Methodist," but the meaning of these terms derives from where I stand in a grander history.

When we apply the discipline of history to our roots, we discover our identity in light of the family as our social fabric. Moreover, we find our identity in the image of a benevolent and providential heavenly father, whose offspring we are. Our earthly concept of family is meant to mirror God's relationality in the vibrant eternal fellowship of Father, Son, and Spirit as well as the expression of his love in creation.[1] Thus, as we *build* our family history and *rebuild* our families today, we are *building into* the life of faith.

In the pages ahead, I broach the respective spheres of faith and family in light of the traditions that shape who we are. Each chapter begins with a reflective portion (drawing on the family traditions that have shaped my life), proceeds with a section critically analyzing key themes, and concludes with points of application.

While I claim that genealogy and family life are best comprehended from a faith-entranced perspective, I hope that this work will also be of benefit to those looking in on the life of faith from the outside. I invite non-religionists interested in their family history to join in this journey of rediscovery.

---

1. For an intriguing discussion of trinitarian fellowship, including a robust depiction (encompassing the maternal figure in the divine family), see McDonough, *The Divine Family*, 121–32.

Introduction

But from everlasting to everlasting the Lord's love is with those who fear him, and his righteousness with their children's children.

—Psalm 103:17, NIV

EACH OF US IS a blend of diverse backgrounds, social experiences, and walks of life. One may call him or herself an Italian, Puerto Rican, Brazilian, Nigerian, or Japanese, or refer to oneself as a Pentecostal, Methodist, Catholic, Jew, or Buddhist. However, the notion that our ethnic or religious identity is somehow homogenous is an illusion. Each person is a mixture, a conglomeration of disparate backgrounds and customs. So much more lies beyond the labels we use to describe ourselves.

Even within a single ethnic group, a person's experiences vary by region and class, among other factors.[1] For example, for those identifying as Irish, it would bear inquiring as to what part of Ireland their ancestry traces. Ireland was restructured politically in 1801, with the northern region grafted into the United Kingdom. Today, the southern region comprises the Republic of Ireland, with a separate government system and currency from the North.[2] Whereas the considerable majority in the Republic of Ireland identify as Catholic (78 percent), under half of Northern Ireland's population is Catholic (41 percent).[3] Thus, it makes a profound difference what

---

1. Stone and King, *Kinship and Gender*. Stone and King delineate the diversity of the United States in light of kinship organization (207–16).

2. Bew, *Ireland: The Politics of Enmity*, 61–63.

3. Central Statistics Office, "Press Statement Census 2016"; Northern Ireland Statistics, "Census 2011," 19.

part of Ireland one's ancestry traces to. If pressed further still, searching for the cities and towns to which someone's family line traces, one would unravel other peculiar customs and traditions.

There remains immense variation among the major branches of the world religions. Today, there are more than 700 different denominations among Pentecostal Christians alone.[4] Consider Judaism, a richly diverse religion. Judaism can be separated into Orthodox, Conservative, Reconstructionist, and Reform branches, in addition to many smaller movements alongside these.[5] Or take Buddhism, which can be divided into multiple schools—Theravada, East Asian, and Tibetan—each comprised of many smaller sub-schools.[6] Each world religion is a heterogeneous cluster of separate and unique traditions. By virtue of one's roots, moreover, each person has been shaped by a litany of experiences and ways of life. Consider the Messianic Jew, someone indebted to both Christian and Jewish sources. My ancestors derived from Catholic Italy, yet identified with Protestantism in America so that subsequent generations must admit the influence of both traditions.

This book proposes a critique of America as the so-called "melting pot," a metaphor corresponding to British playwright Israel Zangwill's idyllic portrait of the United States in a play by the same name.[7] Penned by Zangwill in 1908, the play depicts America as a country teeming with cultural diversity—a symbol of hope and opportunity for people from the most oppressed and disparaging parts of the earth. A land forged on the values of life, liberty, and the pursuit of happiness, the United States promises displaced migrants a chance to rebuild their lives and livelihoods. Indeed, twentieth-century America provided a platform for countless immigrant peoples who, in turn, contributed to the nation's landscape as a multicultural, inclusive land of possibilities. Still, the looming waves of assimilation work to guise, and even suppress, the distinctive customs and beliefs of migrants and refugees, many feeling coerced to conform to American attitudes towards race, the economy, and politics. Inundated with American media, consumerism, and secularity, other groups have forgotten those aspects of their family heritage and background that make them unique.[8]

---

4. Barrett and Johnson, "Global Statistics," 284.
5. Sarna, *American Judaism: A History*, 323–27.
6. Eliade and Adams, *Encyclopedia of Religion*, 440.
7. Zangwill, *Melting-Pot*.
8. Schwartz et al., "Identity Dynamics," 58–59.

THE LIMITS AND UTILITY OF LABELS

I spent most of my life, about twenty-five years, as part of a nondenominational church. Many of the beliefs and principles I live by today were forged in such a setting. Still, to describe oneself as a Methodist and a nondenominational Christian is a contradiction in terms and would leave some scratching their heads. Nondenominational churches have emerged over the past century, in large part, as a reaction to the traditional elements comprising mainstream churches. So, when asked, I call myself a "Pentecostal Methodist."

Ethnic and religious labels are inherently reductionistic. The description "Italian American," for example, or the characterization of myself as a "Pentecostal Methodist," are oversimplifications. Labels fail to represent the diversity inherent within each individual and must be taken with a grain of salt. Néstor Medina, Assistant Professor of Religious Ethics and Culture at the University of Toronto, warns that specific ethnic labels "conceal the rich diversity of peoples subsumed under these classifications."[9] According to Irshad Manji, a professor with the Annenberg Center on Communication Leadership and Policy at the University of Southern California, labels "come with heavy baggage that can distort, or outright hijack, who someone really is."[10] When employed indiscriminately, labels remain unequivocally dangerous.

On the other hand, labels can be useful when applied in a way that helps us acknowledge and more meaningfully talk about our roots. The more serious error is to deny or ignore our differences. Glossing over our differences is one of the chief reasons why we forget our *roots*—the indispensable peculiarities that make each of us who we are.

THE JOURNEY OF REDISCOVERY

This book, in part, chronicles the exploration of my ancestral background. In light of this journey, the first part of this work assesses the value of one's heritage: the faith-based traditions, food culture, and ethnic customs that make each family unique. Subsequent chapters address the significance of identity across the spheres of immigration, social status, race, and religious affiliation. Later portions of the book tackle the more practical arenas of family life, marriage, and mental health. I close with some further

---

9. Medina, *Mestizaje*, x.
10. Manji, *Don't Label Me*, 20.

considerations into how a theistic, faith-entranced approach to genealogy holds promise for cultivating wholeness in our everyday life.

In this work, I use the concept of *re-discovery*, as everyone, self-evidently, has a built-in awareness of their ancestral-identity. However, the tides of acculturation can overwhelm us and cause us, deliberately or unconsciously, to lose sight of our roots and where we come from. As we begin unearthing our origins, we find that the pursuit of our ancestral-identity hinges on a fundamental paradox—to understand who we are, we must look beyond ourselves to those whose legacies we carry on. The journey of rediscovery remains a dynamically relational endeavor. In America, the waves of assimilation have been accompanied by the shift to an increasingly individualistic and depersonalized society. Countless immigrants have come to the shores of the New World, seeking a second chance in the hope of a better way of life for themselves and their posterity. Nevertheless, finding themselves remade in the image of the American way, along the road, they begin to lose sight of the authentic fabric of their identity.

Many American families, recent immigrants and longtime citizens alike, have forgotten that the country is only as strong as its respective parts. Immigration has facilitated a ready supply of labor that has kept the nation afloat while other economies suffer because of unfavorable demographics. Specific skills, particular to each migrant group, have enhanced America's aptitude for innovation, entrepreneurship, and technological advancement.[11] The nation has flowered by bringing together the best of its disparate ethnicities. Regrettably, a degree of comfortability in the decades since the close of the World Wars era has contributed to a preoccupation with private existences.[12] The deluges of Western society continue to erode foundational social institutions, above all, the family. Today, about half of all marriages will end in divorce. Child and domestic abuse remain prominent. The number of single-parent homes rises steadily (nearly fivefold what it was in 1960), and the percent of children born out of wedlock continues to increase.[13]

This book is about the *who* of our roots. The journey of rediscovery pivots on the voices and inspiration of our forebears and, in this way, is an intrinsically personal venture. In a culture of immediate access and virtual social networks—reducing human interaction to "likes," "emoticons," and other notifications delivered via handheld devices—it is easy to set aside

11. National Academies of Sciences, Engineering, and Medicine, *Integration of Immigrants*, 274–75.

12. Ketcham, *Individualism and Public Life*, vii–viii.

13. Schramm and Allen, "Divorce and Religion," 366; Schroth, "Child Abuse," 178–79; Kte'pi, "Social History of American Families," 1241; Livingston, "Changing Profile of Unmarried Parents."

those values that build genuine interpersonal relationships. Sharing our latest status update over social media is hardly a substitute for meaningful conversation and quality time in the company of loved ones and friends. Embracing our roots means building into the lives of those we care about and learning to appreciate those who have built into ours. The rise in the popularity of genealogy databases such as Ancestry.com and FamilySearch suggests a national interest in exploring our origins. Still, such resources, accessed chiefly through electronic devices, will prove most beneficial when utilized alongside more personal avenues of inquiry. Thumbing through inherited correspondences and photographs, for example, provides a rare and more earnest glimpse into the lives of our ancestors, living and deceased.

WHO WE WERE MADE TO BE: REREADING BIBLICAL GENEALOGY

The pages ahead provide a platform to reconnect, reconsider, and rediscover who we were *made to be*. I must admit my theistic leanings, as they inform my perspective in crucial ways. As a *theist*, I believe who we were made to be points to the design and purpose of a creator. Foremost, we were made to reflect the character of God. Each one of us bears the imprint of our Creator, the image of God (Lat., *imago Dei*). As we find in the opening chapter of Scripture: "Then God said, 'Let us make humankind in our image, according to our likeness'" (Gen 1:26, NRSV). The use of the plural, "let us make" (Heb., `asah), implies the *Trinity* (lit., the "three-in-one"). God's image encompasses both his *diversity* (threeness) and *unity* (oneness). In this way, humanity is meant to radiate God's character both in the beauty of our diversity (culturally, ethnically, and religiously) and in our shared identity as bearers of the imago Dei. The dynamically present and involved Creator God surpasses that of the *deist*, for whom God merely set the world in motion only to, thereafter, leave it to its own devices. I invite the deist to consider that the same God who *made* us also aims to *embrace* us, even as we embrace who we were made to be.

More than a few verses in the Bible are devoted to genealogies: Genesis chapters 4 and 5 detail the family line of Noah, beginning with Adam and Eve; Genesis 10 and 11 outline the lineage of Abraham; and the ancestry of Jesus appears in the first chapter of Matthew. From a biblical perspective, the value of genealogy is illustrated in the parallel in Genesis between the creation of Adam in the imago Dei (1:26–27) and Adam begetting a son, Seth, in his likeness: "When Adam had lived one hundred thirty years, he became the father of a son in his likeness, according to his image, and named him Seth" (5:3, NRSV). In this way, Adam and his progeny trace explicitly to God, the father of all humankind. The author of Genesis depicts humanity's creation in terms of a loving father establishing and looking after his family, ensuring his favor from one generation to the next.[14] Noah's genealogy in chapter 10 (the Table of Nations) offers an all-embracing portrait of God's fatherhood over the many (seventy) nations represented in the list. Moreover, God is specifically shown to be the father of Abraham and his descendants, to whom Yahweh's original blessing will be renewed (12:1–3).[15]

From one generation to the next, the unfolding of redemptive history reveals the providence and care of a loving heavenly father. God's plan and purpose culminate in the story of Jesus. In the metanarrative of redemption, the genealogy of Jesus (Matt 1:2–16) unites all of Scripture, old and new. Jesus's tie to Abraham and David represents the inheritance of God's original blessing. Furthermore, the inclusion of five women (Tamar, Rahab, Ruth, Bathsheba, and Mary)—all (except Mary) with Gentile connections—demonstrates Jesus's Messiahship not only over Israel but for all the nations.[16] Genealogy comprises a distinctive part of the biblical canon, conveying something indispensable about God's character and plan.

WHY AND HOW TO READ THIS BOOK

Perhaps you have lost a family member and wish to consider their legacy anew, or you want to reconnect with other loved ones grieving the same loss. Perhaps you are a parent and want to reflect on how you were brought up to inform how you will raise children of your own. Perhaps you're one of the millions of Americans who have lost touch and live out each day trying to "find yourself." Rediscovering our roots opens a new window into our family heritage and adds new meaning to everyday family life.

While providing a personal glimpse into my journey of rediscovery, this work also serves an instructional end. The book utilizes three heuristic tools: a how-to guide for building your family history (appendix A); my family tree, as an example for tracing your generational lines (appendix B); and chapter reflection questions. These are exercises for everyone. For example, as a nation of immigrants, every American is an "ethnic" American and stands to gain from considering the people and places they come from and the customs and beliefs that make them, and their ancestral line, unique. Even those who have veered from the family and faith traditions

14. Sailhamer, *Pentateuch as Narrative*, 117–18.
15. Sailhamer, *Pentateuch as Narrative*, 130–31.
16. Blomberg, *Jesus and the Gospels*, 233.

of their upbringing stand to learn immensely from building (tracing and writing) their forebears' history. The reflection questions provide a guide for thinking critically about the themes of the corresponding chapter. You may wish to keep a journal or pencil in your thoughts as you work through them.

The places we come from (the *where* question) and circumstances surrounding our roots (the *what* question) remain peripheral to the people we come from (the *who* question). By rediscovering our roots—considering again the path our forebears walked—we will be better able to make sense of and, as fitting, reconsider the course of our lives today. Learning about the ancestral-identity that makes each of us unique illumines a sure path forward while reaffirming the rich cultural diversity on which America was founded. Moreover, as we comprehend the people and places we descend from, we confront anew the character of a loving heavenly father, who holds each generation of our family line intact, promising to bless and establish the offspring of all those who fear him.

PART I

Valuing Our Heritage

1

Sunday Dinner

Making an Ethno-Faith Tradition

So then, a sabbath rest still remains for the people of God; for those who enter God's rest also cease from their labors as God did from his.
—Hebrews 4:9–10, NRSV

THE DOORBELL RINGS. MOM calls out from the top of the stairs, "Grammy and Grandpa are here!" My younger brother and I pause our video game in the basement and rush upstairs to greet them. We open the front door, reach out, and embrace Grammy and Grandpa with a hug and kiss.

As Grammy leans in to kiss my cheek, she utters the word *"pace"* (Italian for "peace"). I head outside to help carry in the plates of food—sauce, meatballs, fresh veggies, and deserts—to go alongside the ravioli already simmering on the stove.

Growing up as an Italian American and a Pentecostal, few aspects of life were more certain than our Sunday routine. Each week culminated around that one awaited and precious day. Sundays offered a sense of continuity to the ebb and flow, the hustle and bustle, of everyday American life. After moving on all cylinders the rest of the week, everyone—Dad, Mom, grandparents, and kids alike—cherished the joy and constancy this one day of the week afforded. Sunday was a day to unwind and reset, to be nourished in body and heart.

REST FOR THE WEARY AMERICAN

Sunday was the day we rested because our family would, inevitably, fill the remainder of our waking hours with productivity. Perhaps the quality most American about us was our trenchant work ethic, passed down from our migrant forebears. If there was one attribute about the country we took pride in above all else, it was the working spirit that built America from the ground up. My parents (and grandparents and great-grandparents before them) knew there was no such thing as a free ticket when it came to pursuing the American dream. A lesson learned early on was that achieving that dream would entail immense and even painstaking effort. In America, my grandparents' and great-grandparents' working lives on both sides of the family centered on the ministry. And until the denomination to which my family devoted their lives began to fund ministerial offices, this meant holding multiple jobs to make ends meet. In addition to his pastoral work, my maternal grandfather was a foreman in a printing press. Carrying on the rich artisanal tradition of Italy, two of my great-grandfathers were mosaicists.

Dad and Mom set the tone for our household, raising the bar to a seemingly unattainable, nevertheless, estimable height. At one point, we had a running total going of Dad's sick days home from work. He spent forty-one years with the same west-side Syracuse dental practice. I am not sure where the total stands today. Back when we kept the tally alive, Dad had twenty years or more under his belt, but you could still count the total number of sick days on one hand. Mom excelled in the versatility with which she moved seamlessly from one avenue of work to another. With a degree in education, fresh out of graduate school, Mom took up teaching for her profession. After carrying on the work she loved for many years while putting Dad through dental school, Mom took leave to raise four kids. Having three kids of my own today makes me appreciate all the more the energy Mom spent building into our lives. In due time, she donned her teaching cap again and returned to the career she loved.

If the effort put forward on their day jobs wasn't enough, Mom and Dad juggled their time caring for a large extended family, church involvement, and nurturing me and my siblings' extracurricular activities. Reaching the bar raised by our parents meant not only excelling at school but spreading our wings in other areas—notably, church, sports, and music. We successfully fit in many such activities on Saturdays. After the workweek concluded, there was always more left to accomplish on weekends. A typical Saturday in the Palma household entailed soccer league in the morning, piano practice in the afternoon, and play rehearsal at the church in the evening.

Sunday afternoon couldn't have come soon enough. Sunday morning continued the busyness of the previous days of the week. But it was a different kind of busyness. At church each week, we rededicated our time, efforts, and involvements under the banner of corporate worship. Nine o'clock Sunday school, followed by the main service at ten thirty, was a time to refocus and reconsider the purpose behind the week-in, week-out hustle and bustle.

FEASTING WITH LA FAMIGLIA

Sunday afternoon together was the capstone of each week. To accommodate the extended family of grandparents, aunts, and uncles, we brought out the table leaf (sometimes "leaves" if the cousins joined us). Little intervening time passed between church and "dinner" (as Italian Americans refer to the midday Sunday meal). Typically, everyone arrived directly after the morning service, appearing in their Sunday finest: suits, dresses (sometimes the ladies wore caps), and other formal wear. Everyone greeted one another with a kiss, known in Italian Pentecostal circles as the *bacio di pace* ("kiss of peace"),[17] after the well-attested New Testament precedent: "Greet one another with a kiss of love. Peace to all of you who are in Christ" (1 Pet 5:14, NRSV).[18] We rotated Sunday dinner between three homes: ours on Syracuse's east side, my paternal grandparents' on the west side, and my maternal grandparents' on the north side. While my grandparents were shoo-ins to attend as well as our dear Aunt Esther and Uncle Dominick, depending on the week and location, any number of others were invited. Occasionally we were joined by my cousin Alma and her kids, Aunt Febe and Uncle Eugene, Aunt Fay, Aunt Helen, and the list goes on. Often, we invited our friends from church. Irrespective of their ethnic background, they tasted the Italian cultural experience for those few hours on Sunday afternoon, heaps of olive oil and tomato sauce in all.

After brief greetings and embrace, we made our way to the table to sit in our prearranged seats. Ordinarily, the family head led off the meal

---

17. Unless otherwise noted, all translations of Italian are my own.

18. Also referred to in the NRSV and NIV as a "holy kiss" (see Rom 16:16; 1 Cor 16:20; 2 Cor 13:12; and 1 Thess 5:26); St. Augustine speaks of the holy kiss as a sign of peace in one of his Easter sermons. Augustine, Sermon 227; the liturgical significance of the "kiss of peace" can be traced through Medieval and Modern Christianity. See Thurston, "Kiss."

with a prayer—my dad or one of my grandfathers (in Italian homes, "headship" is allotted to the presiding male). Following our "amens" and "thank you, Lords" in unison, the grand feast ensued. The full four-course meal started with an appetizer—typically a fruit dish (my favorites being mandarin oranges and fruit cocktail with a cherry on top). Next up was the salad dish. While the salad tasted notably different among the three homes, the ingredients were always of the essential Italian variety. Any disparity was owing chiefly to some proportional difference in the amount of olive oil and red wine vinegar. On my dad's side of the family, Grandma Palma, whom we affectionately referred to as *Nonna* (Italian for grandma), always errored on the side of more vinegar. Alongside other fixings, the dressing complemented the freshest pickings of Romaine lettuce. My maternal grandparents grew red, plump, juicy tomatoes in their backyard, which also served as the base of a fresh pasta sauce we prepared as a family using a machine press.

The main course was soon in coming. From the prayer to the main dish, there was an unmistakable shift in prestige. In Italian homes, the cook possesses an indisputable honor, one that subverts Western stereotypes about the domestication of women. As the meal unfolds, the scale of prestige tilts firmly in favor of the household matriarch. The woman who knows how to cook (and in our family, they all did!) is considered a master chef. Nonna's claim to fame was her spinach macaroni. I realize that the typical kid's reaction to a food with the name "spinach" in it is probably "yuck," tempered by an assertive "no thank you." Yet, I never consciously thought about it nor cared for that matter, that there was spinach in the meal. The macaroni was simply delicious. I don't know precisely how much spinach was in the dish, but it gave the meal its characteristic green hue. The pasta itself, which Nonna always handmade, was a wide linguini type—several times the girth of your typical spaghetti pasta but flattened. The dish was prepared in a butter-parmesan sauce, mixed to perfection. I think her recipe survives somewhere but could scarcely be duplicated with the craft and exquisite balance of portions with which Nonna prepared it. Plus, it had the bonus of being bona fide healthy for you (it was spinach after all).

I mentioned the tomatoes—homegrown and home-pressed. The machine press helped turn the tomatoes into a superlative pasta sauce. It was a tag-team effort producing the sauce. Grandpa grew, harvested, and pressed the tomatoes, and Grandma whirled them. The final product was a veritable feat with just the right mixture of ingredients and garden-fresh homemade taste. No pasta dish is complete without fresh tomato sauce. My mom pioneered homemade sauce-making here in America. She grew up in Queens, deprived of access to juicy tomatoes families of suburban, upstate New York enjoy. For the first time, with the move to Syracuse, she could pick any fresh fruit or vegetable she wanted from the local farm.

The sauce-making was quite an elaborate process. After picking the tomatoes, they had to be washed, cut up, placed in large pans, and cooked down to food consistency. They were then fed through the press several times to exact all of the tomato seeds and skins. Next, the tomato juice was transferred to sterilized jars and placed on the shelf. Finally, mixed with just the right combination of spices, the juice was transformed into that superb sauce. My folks practiced this technique for years with a manual press before Dad found a machine for the press crank and automated the process. When my grandparents started harvesting their tomatoes in the garden, my mom gave them the press. So, as the tradition carried on, our Sunday dinner was always complemented by the freshest homegrown, homemade tomato sauce you could find.

Still, what the sauce encompassed stole the show every time. My mom's stepmother, whom we affectionately called Grandma Santa, prepared the finest meatballs known this side of the Mississippi. I have tasted my share of meatballs over the years, but none match the combination of flavor, texture, and satisfaction of Grandma Santa's. After she passed away, bless her soul, we experimented with a host of different brands and recipes, but nothing measured up. The closest we came was meatballs from a local Italian eatery—"Ashodi's." The Ashodi recipe was quite good, but still a distant second to Grandma Santa's. In later years, when we resorted to Ashodi's, it cheered our hearts, reminding us of our beloved Grandma Santa and her unrivaled meatballs.

When it was our home's turn to host, one could look forward to the array of dishes Mom would whip up: my favorites being cavatelli, ravioli, and stuffed shells. Mom's stuffed shells would be considered a delicacy on any restaurant menu. They resemble cheese ravioli, except the cheese is packed into a large, cone-shaped pasta, with the proportion of cheese to pasta tilted slightly in favor of the cheese.

Mom's famous stuffed shells comprise a meal rich in flavor, texture, and protein. An assortment of cheeses makes up the scrumptious center: the most prominent being ricotta, with a touch of Locatelli and Parmesan. And the pasta, known in Italian as *conchiglie*, really is shell-shaped (enclosed at each end). The pasta is filled from the underside with the cheese blend and then wrapped up. Its exterior is serrated with shell-like crevices, evenly encompassing each side, allowing the sauce to adhere to the pasta. The dish is aptly named, given both the shape of the pasta and its felt effect. It is impossible to eat my mom's stuffed shells without feeling "stuffed" yourself. Always feeling full afterward is owing to the cheese ensemble and that, after the first shell, one easily inclines to another and then another, and so on. At the close of the meal, one can expect to feel quite stuffed with stuffed shells. Any timidity in requesting a second helping was neutralized by the refrain—repeated on all occasions at each home with little exception—*mangia tutto, mangia* ("eat everything, eat"). So naturally, we helped ourselves to another serving.

Another dish of Mom's I have always enjoyed is her manicotti. It's a close race for me—between the manicotti and stuffed shells. When I inquired of her about the manicotti ingredients, she shared the story behind her recipe. Manicotti is comprised of some of the same ingredients as stuffed shells, particularly the cheese, yet it is prepared differently and with a uniquely shaped pasta. *Manicotti* (literally meaning "little sleeves") is a tube-like pasta, open on each end. Unlike stuffed shells, the cheese is not loaded into the pasta but instead placed on a pasta base and rolled.

Just after my parents were married, Mom wanted to find the best manicotti recipe with which to impress her new mother- and father-in-law for their first visit to my folks' place. Mom and Dad were renting an upstairs garage apartment from an older Italian couple and friends of the family, the Campaniles. Mrs. Campanile was known for her elegant manicotti and graciously passed the recipe on to my mom. Mom proceeded to prepare the meal according to the recipe—everything right from scratch. After my grandma tasted the dish, she remarked, "This is delicious. Where'd you get the recipe?" Relieved by the positive response, Mom explained how she came by it. Grandma was taken aback and then, with a look of contentment, replied, "Oh, that's my recipe. I shared it with Mrs. Campanile." And so, Italian Americans often travel in small circles. Over the years, Mom has adapted the recipe to her liking.

After we finished the main dish, there was little room left for dessert. Ordinarily, we disbanded from the table to digest before being summoned back an hour-or-so later to finish the full course. We occasionally enjoyed a fine pie, although typically of the American sort: apple, blueberry, and cherry varieties. The Italian desserts came out in force for the holidays, highlighted by Mom's renowned Tortoni—French vanilla ice cream mixed with rum and whipped cream and decorated with a chopped cherry. Nonna treated us to her Italian anise cookies from time to time—a soft, cake-like, licorice-flavored desert covered in sprinkles. Following dessert, the adults often remained at the table for a coffee-espresso pick-me-up and some hearty conversation.

After the main course, and again following dessert, the guys migrated to the couch and recliner in the family room. While the ladies could be found congregating in the dining or living room for conversation, for the rest of us, from the close of the meal onward, Sunday afternoon proceeded with the favored American pastime of watching sports. It was time to unwind while enjoying whatever seasonal sport was airing, with the schedule rotating between football, basketball, and baseball. This typical wind-down routine was the norm for my dad, my two brothers, myself, and the granddads. We have always been a big sports family. My siblings and I each played our share of sports for the school team and many years as two-season athletes. Of course, we interspersed our sports-watching with a relished catnap. I was lucky to last through the first quarter or inning of a game before dosing off. Our napping translated into many half-awake goodbyes to departing family or, when elsewhere besides our house, another catnap in the car on the way back home.

Come evening, after the cheers, hugs, and goodbyes, everyone returned to their respective abodes across the greater-Syracuse area with their tummies full and hearts fuller. It's hard to think we could contemplate more food on the same day, or even the same week. But being the good Italians that we were, when five-thirty or six o'clock rolled around, we gathered in the kitchen again, although this time informally and on our own accord. Our second dinner (at traditional "supper" time) was typically on the smaller side: a trifling compared to the afternoon feast, usually consisting of a no-hassle pop-in or re-cook of leftovers from the banquet earlier that day. Rarely did we sit down again formally at the table, and more often than not, our meal returned with us to our designated stations as we finished watching the ball game.

A DAY WE CHERISHED

At the close of our Sunday routine, we had come full circle—refreshed and reconstituted to face the week ahead. Losing ourselves in the affable graces of corporate fellowship at church and home around the table, we were able to distance ourselves from the hustle and bustle of the week. Our daily and trivial concerns were baptized into the gravitas of solidarity with loved ones and delectable food. We awoke the next day, nourished, restored, and ready to take on the grind, one week at a time.

Was it legalism that made us refrain from work and observe our Sabbath of repose? To this day, I set aside Sunday as a time for family, church, and rest. I do my best to wrap up teaching, publications, conference prep, and other professional responsibilities on Friday or Saturday. Once in a blue moon, with a Monday-imposed deadline, I make an exception, but that's after taking in at least some of the family, church, and rest time that I need. Sunday remains my favorite day of the week. Growing up, we never regretted that we filled our time with things besides work on Sundays. And we didn't live this way out of a sense of duty or compulsion. It wasn't until college, when I was on my own and had a choice, that I even acknowledged there was such a thing as a biblical law about keeping a day of rest. As Exodus 20 states:

> Remember the sabbath day, and keep it holy. Six days you shall labor and do all your work. But the seventh day is a sabbath to the LORD your God; you shall not do any work—you, your son or your daughter, your male or female slave, your livestock, or the alien resident in your towns (vv. 8–10, NRSV).

I knew the commandment was there but had never given it much thought. We always "remembered" our Sabbath day of rest—it was just the way we lived.

The Hebrew term from which we derive the English word "Sabbath" is *shabbath*, literally meaning to "repose" or "desist from exertion."[19] For the Jewish people, the Sabbath is a time for eating, singing, conversation, and relaxation, away from school and work pressures. This tradition likely reaches back to before the Bible was written. There is precedent for a Sabbath-day-like observance in the ancient Babylonian *Shabbatum*, the "day of the full moon," on which it was believed that the moon stood still. On this day, considered "a day of rest of the heart" for the gods, the Babylonian gods were thought to be particularly disposed to showing mercy and favor and were thus "pacified" with ceremonies.[20] For the Jewish people, the Sabbath falls on a Saturday (beginning sundown on Friday and extending through sundown Saturday). It is considered a day of joy, typified for many by song at the communal Saturday noontime and late afternoon meals. Eighteenth- and nineteenth-century Eastern European Jewish families popularized the custom of setting aside the best food, wine, and clothing during the week to be used as part of the Sabbath-day celebration at the week's end.[21]

My family always observed a day of rest. It just so happened that it fell on a Sunday. Could it have been another day of the week? Some people go to church on Saturday. I am friends with several ministers who work on Sundays and thus opt for Mondays or another day as their Sabbath. For us, Sunday was the best fit. The practice became an ingrained part of our lifestyle. However, keeping a Sabbath was never something we felt like we *had* to do. It was never something where, after meeting our rest quota for

---

19. Strong, *Dictionary of the Hebrew Bible*, 112.
20. Jastrow, *Hebrew and Babylonian Traditions*, 148–49.
21. Cardozo, *Jewish Family Celebrations*, 2–8.

the week, we placed a checkmark on our list of spiritual observances to be kept. Moreover, we never referred to it as "the Sabbath." In truth, I do not recall my parents ever insisting that I refrain from schoolwork on Sundays. It's just that everyone valued rest and family time over work on this one day of the week. Having our Sunday of repose was something longed for and cherished, and, for that reason alone, we "kept it holy."

Reflection Questions:

- What are some faith traditions your ancestors practiced? Do you still observe these today? How do these traditions reflect qualities that make you and your family unique?
- Do you set aside an extended block of time each week for worship, rest, and leisure? If not, what prevents you? What day in your weekly routine would work best as a Sabbath? You can always start small—with a half day—and build from there.

2

I May Not Look It, but I'm "FBI"

Towards a Healthy Ethnocentrism

For the Lord does not see as mortals see; they look on the outward appearance, but the Lord looks on the heart.
—1 Samuel 16:7, NRSV

SOME WILL RECALL THE World Wrestling Entertainment tag team during the nineties and two-thousands showcasing Italian Americans by the stage names Little Guido and Big Sal E. Graziano. The iconic duo popularized the phrase "Full Blooded Italians." Others will have seen the t-shirt brand featuring the abbreviation "FBI" in large bold caps—displayed in the green, white, and red colors of the Italian flag—with "Full Blooded Italian" written-out beneath. If you are an FBI, it is something you take pride in and want others to know. It's important to be proud of our ethnic background. One of the chief obstacles to having pride in our roots is when others make assumptions about us based on our appearance: our stature, skin tone, hair color, and other features. Feeling judged by others, or ourselves, can reinforce stereotypes and perpetuate conscious indifference, regret, or ignorance about our ancestral heritage.

PRIDE IN THE LAND WE COME FROM

There are still some full-blooded Italians in America today, although far fewer than during the years following the mass migration of the late nineteenth and early twentieth centuries. Over 2 million Italians immigrated to America between 1901 and 1910, compared to less than 60,000 between 1941 and 1950—a more than 97 percent drop-off.[1] In tandem with the forces of acculturation, the severe decrease of Italian immigration has curbed the reservoir of Americans whose ancestry, on all sides, traces directly to Italy. It is even less common to be a third-generation immigrant and still have maintained "full-blooded" status. Intermarriage between Italian immigrants and other Americans has increased among succeeding generations, alongside the number of offspring who are a mixture of Italian and one or more of the medley of ethnicities comprising the nation today. The blending of ethnicities is a natural and, arguably, healthy result of acculturation. Intermarriage, specifically when both parties feel comfortable retaining aspects of their ancestral background, is a positive outworking of multiculturalism.[2]

Nevertheless, here I am, an FBI, three generations since my ancestors stepped foot on American soil. My great-grandparents entered America during the Great Migration of Italians, spanning from approximately 1870 to 1920. During this mass migration, they arrived with scores of other Italians, more than any other period in US history. These eager migrants sought the fortunes and freedoms of the New World. I am the prodigy of these hopeful journeyers, who overcame estrangement and marginalization in America's city enclaves, en route to laying hold of all that the New World promised.[3]

The Italian migrant's typical profile was that of the agrarian *contadini* (peasants) from southern Italy. *Contadini* had been relegated by country and church to the bottom-rung of society. In Italy, the peasantry lived as subsistent farm laborers, working the fields while living on the property of absentee landowners.[4] The *contadini* clawed their way from one room tenant homes, scrounging whatever funds they could to meet emigration demands. In their passage to America, peasants faced harsh conditions and the persistent threat of disease. As immigrants, they endured the loss of familiar surroundings, impediments to acquiring food and shelter, and the possibility of losing one or both parents.[5]

1. Spickard, *Almost All Aliens*, 293.
2. Schwartz et al., "Identity Dynamics," 58–59.
3. Handlin, *Uprooted*, 104–10.
4. Gans, "Boston's West End," 280.
5. Berrol, *Growing Up American*, 1.

Most Italian migrants were young men who, having left family behind, intended only a sojourn. After earning enough wealth, they planned to return to their families in Italy with the bounty.[6] The unforeseen reality for many, however, was the beginning of a new life in America. Finding, in addition to steady work, a fresh and inviting ecclesial network, my forebears opted to dig their roots in America. While most returned to Italy later on, they eventually made their way back to the New World, although this time with their families in tow, ready to pursue American citizenship and build a new life.

So yes, I am proud to be a full-blooded Italian. The phrase harkens to the strivings of my ancestors who, amid repression and marginalization, never wavered in making a name for themselves. They worked diligently so that I, in turn, might live well, with perhaps more opportunities than those whose legacies I carry on. I have an FBI shirt—it was a gift. I rarely wear it in public, simply because I am not one to draw attention to myself. Then again, for those who do, I applaud them. If we can take pride in our hometown sports team, why should we feel shame for having pride in our forebears? Taking pride in my ethnicity allows me to carry on the legacy of the migrant *contadini,* who made the opportunities I enjoy today possible. I laud my ancestors, who voyaged beyond the urban ghettos into the hinterlands of America, to build a new life for generations to come.

A number of circumstances had to converge so that I might be able to boast, as I do today, about my full-blooded Italianness. One is the city in which I was born and raised. Some US cities house one or more "Little Italies." These statuettes of Italian society shelter ethnic identity to ease immigrant family resettlement in the New World.[7] The city I grew up in, Syracuse, had several Little Italies. Today, the county I belonged to, Onondaga, has about 75,000 Italian Americans, approximately 16 percent of the population.[8] The name itself, "Syracuse" (Siracusa in Italian), derives from a city on Sicily's eastern coast. Migrant Italians first entered Syracuse during the construction of the West Shore railroad in the eighteen-eighties. Already by 1897, nearly 5,000 Italian migrants lived in Syracuse.[9] The city served as a strategic stopping point between New York City (the arrival site for most émigrés) and the Great Lakes. In 1910, the Big Apple boasted an Italian diasporic population of more than 340,000, larger than any other

---

6. Mangione and Morreale, *La storia,* 328.

7. On the role of Little Italies, see Garroni, "Interpreting Little Italies," 163–64.

8. US Census Bureau, "American Community Survey," under "Onondaga County, New York."

9. Loos, "Syracuse's Foreign Born Population," 28.

city in the world.¹⁰ After porting in New York City, some of my ancestors settled beyond the Great Lakes in Chicago. Yet, their summons to ministry brought my forebears to Syracuse years later, the first arriving in 1920 to lead a church on the city's westside.

Syracuse's demographics were partially responsible for how my parents came together, nearly a century after the start of the Great Migration that ushered my ancestors to the New World. My folks wed in 1972. Their shared experience growing up in the church also contributed to their union. Both Mom and Dad were pastor's kids in a very Italian Pentecostal denomination. They met as sixteen-year-olds at an annual convention for the Christian Church of North America.

BEYOND APPEARANCES

If someone took me at face value, one might very well question my FBI status, and such suspicion would be understandable. I stand among the third generation of Italian Americans in my family, reaching back to my ancestors' arrival in the late nineteenth century, meaning a "pure" line had been preserved for nearly a century with the birth of my siblings and me. To be a full-blooded Italian this many generations later is remarkable considering America's diversity and how common intermarriage is today among the country's disparate ethnicities. Since the 1967 *Loving v. Virginia* Supreme Court case, forbidding anti-miscegenation laws, the United States' rate of intermarriage has steadily increased (it rose 28 percent from 2000 to 2010).¹¹

Moreover, my outlying features do not lend themselves to the common caricatures of Italian nationality. The typical profile of the Italian male is someone with dark skin, hair, and eyes and, according to one study, standing 174 cm (about five foot eight and one-half inch) tall.¹² These features resemble southern Italians, in particular, comprising the decisive majority of Italian migration to America. Qualities like shortness of stature and lack of physical strength were commonly attributed to southerners in the early Italian immigration era. Generally-speaking, Italian migrants were smaller and weaker than the average American. Studies suggest such "stunted development" is commonplace for peoples coming from a long line of generations who once lived in isolation together in small communities.¹³ I am relatively light-skinned, burning readily from over-exposure to the

10. Baily, *Immigrants in the Lands of Promise*, 58.
11. Csizmadia, "Interracial Marriage," 756–57.
12. Krul et al., "Measured Weight, Height and Body Mass," 415.
13. Sowell, *Ethnic America*, 114.

sun. My hair is light brown, my eyes greenish-blue, and I stand at six foot three. So I can't blame others for the second-looks I receive when I tell them I am a full-blooded Italian.

I inherited many of the same features as my dad. On the other hand, my mom, with darker traits, is closer to the stereotypical Italian profile. It behooves me to carry a picture of her close in hand as proof of my ethnicity. Even still, someone could infer, "It seems you have just inherited your dad's traits, and he must be from the very northern regions of Italy." Yet, it is not that simple. The majority of my ancestry traces to the South. My dad is equal parts southern and northern, while my mom's roots derive entirely from the South. Yes, I am tall, light-haired, and light-skinned. However, if one judged me at face value, they would miss the truth about who I am and where I come from. Similarly, if one viewed all southern Italians the same based on their outlying characteristics, they would miss the big picture. If Samuel took the sons of Jesse at face value, Eliab, instead of David, might have been crowned King of Israel. As we read in 1 Samuel 16:

> But the LORD said to Samuel, "Do not look on his appearance or on the height of his stature, because I have rejected him; for the LORD does not see as mortals see; they look on the outward appearance, but the LORD looks on the heart" (v. 7, NRSV).

Although Eliab's brawn made him appear more suitable for kingship at face value, God saw something beyond the surface that would lead to David's establishment as perhaps the greatest king in the history of the Israelite people. If we want to glimpse the vantage point of God for our lives and relationships, we must remind ourselves that outlying features are never the measure of our worth.

DEVELOPING A HEALTHY ETHNOCENTRISM

I take pride in my ethnic background. Does that make me ethnocentric? Well, not in the sense that I laud Italians as superior to other ethnicities. There is a fine line between prizing where someone comes from, on the one hand, and privileging one's ethnic group as better than another, on the other hand. I am proud of where I come from and have no trouble admitting it. The alternatives to ethnocentrism are bleak, to say the least. One option is not to care about where and who we come from. *Indifference* about our roots can lead to an underdeveloped or, perhaps worse, a false sense of identity. Another alternative is to *regret* our ancestral background. Both options tread the path of futility.

Concerning the second alternative—regret—everyone can find something lamentable about their origins if they look hard enough. People of Scandinavian descent, for example, might very well trace their ancestry back to the medieval Vikings. While they may regret the fact that their ancestors raided and pillaged towns across vast areas of Europe, despite stereotypes, the Vikings also possessed keen ingenuity as avid explorers and navigators of the open seas. It is for the latter reason that, according to one list, about 90 US high schools and colleges have Vikings as their team mascot (to this, one could add the NFL franchise the Minnesota Vikings).[14] I may have cause to regret the fact that some of my family lineage belonged to the Mafia (though I have not yet made this connection). Still, whither the value of wallowing in regret? As depicted in films like the Godfather series and Goodfellas, Mafia members can possess admirable traits—devotion to family and commitment to a common cause. Might such attributes, while once misappropriated within the context of a crime syndicate, in another setting be put toward some socially-amicable cause?

There is one other way we can approach our ethnic background—the path of *ignorance*. Some simply have no idea where their roots trace. Such unawareness is not uncommon among Americans. The American "melting pot," although fostering unity on one level, has eroded for many any sense of what it originally was that brought their forebears to the nation. Many American schools, intent on turning "little aliens" into "little citizens," have, in the process, lost sight of the educational value of cultural diversity.[15] The people and places someone comes from offer certain clues into why they feel, think, and act in specific ways. Rediscovering our cultural identity helps us understand and nurture our unique gifts; indeed, a healthy critique of the "melting pot" analogy impresses us to stop and reconsider our roots.

Blind assimilation to any culture causes us to lose sight of the pieces of our identity that make us unique and valuable to society. From a Honduran immigrant family, actress America Ferrera describes how she learned to stop "shedding pieces of her identity" while trying to assimilate to American culture. In *American Like Me*, Ferrera illustrates that it was precisely her distinctive complexion ("brownness") and "ethnic-looking" features that landed her career-making screen roles.[16] She enchanted her audiences and furthered her opportunities because of her so-called "un-American" qualities. At the same time, there are some aspects of American culture

---

14. "Viking Mascot School List," Ranker, https://www.ranker.com/list/viking-mascot-school-list/reference.

15. Berrol, *Growing Up American*, 31.

16. Ferrera, *American Like Me*, 303.

from which immigrants could stand to benefit. My ancestors were drawn to the industrial spirit of the nation. America's thriving modern climate was something they wished to adopt; however, not at the expense of their cultural uniqueness.

The love of my life is also an ethnic American. I married a first-generation French American (and it was the best decision I ever made!). While we share certain European sensibilities—we both cherish our midday siesta and favor a Mediterranean diet—there is plenty about us that differs by virtue of our ethnic roots. I could persuade her to become more like me (and have pasta every night), but that would imply I have nothing to learn from her "Frenchness" (and I love the occasional Quiche for dinner). The better path forward is affirming my wife in her interests so that she can rediscover all that's valuable about being French (and everything I love about her that's French). Being a little ethnocentric about our roots is okay, as long as we leave room for and encourage the ethnocentricity of others.

So as I consider my ethnic roots, among the alternatives—conscious indifference, regret, or ignorance—I have chosen another more productive avenue. This path entails *rediscovery*—unearthing those aspects that are good and admirable about my background and consciously building on them. If I am guilty of ethnocentrism by cherishing those qualities that make me unique, then I am okay with being ethnocentric. If viewing other cultures from the vantage point of my *Italianità* (Italianness) makes me an ethnocentrist, then so be it. Each of us sees others through a prism colored by our roots—the traditions, places, foods, and enjoyments that make us who we are. In this sense, all of us are predisposed to ethnocentricity. The better path forward is to acknowledge our inherent ethnocentrism and embrace our roots.

Reflection Questions:

- Do you ever feel like others make assumptions about you based on your outward appearance? Do you ever judge yourself in this way?
- Who among your family members, immediate or distant, can you speak with to learn more about your true ethnic identity?
- Do you take pride in your ancestral roots? Why or why not? In the interest of cultivating "healthy" ethnocentrism, identify aspects about your heritage you can take pride in.

3

Enjoying an Afternoon Siesta

It is useless for you to work so hard
from early morning until late at night,
anxiously working for food to eat;
for God gives rest to his loved ones.

—Psalm 127:2, NLT

WHEN CHANGE IS A GOOD THING

It was the last year of middle school—the eighth grade. The student yearbook committee announced they would feature a "Most Likely To" award section for the graduating class. Every student filled out a ballot. On the last day of the year, after awaiting the big reveal, I sifted through the book to find my name listed under the category, "Most Likely Never to Change." As everyone was collecting yearbook signatures, a friend approached me with a grin on his face. He leaned in and, quite awkwardly, sniffed me. With a perplexed look, he remarked, "I don't get it. If you never change your clothes. . . I'd expect you'd have body odor?"

I chuckled and said, "That's not what the award is about." Unless I am mistaken (and all these years, my Middle School class has been laughing at me for poor hygiene), the award is not a reference to changing one's clothes but rather intended for the person "Most Likely Never to Change," that is, his character.

For children and young adults, "not changing" is an estimable quality. Change implies capitulating to the world and altering how one thinks, acts, and looks. As the child moves out beyond the familiar surroundings of home and the nurture of parents, the world and culture around them exert an unmistakable pressure. As the child advances through the school system, the expectations of peers and teachers begin to change them. When change elicits thoughts, feelings, and behaviors that conflict with a person's values and customs, it can have a detrimental effect. For this reason, the person who resists the pressure to conform—whose values and identity remain firmly intact—is lauded as someone of proven character. So then, I am grateful for the "Most Likely Never to Change" award, as it suggests that others esteemed me as a person of character.

The simple reality is that people change. For adults, change can mean something entirely different than for a child. When adults look back on their life, they often see how different they are from the free-spirited child of their youth. Adults have the advantage of hindsight, which can lead to wanting to *change back* to the values and customs of their upbringing. There is nothing wrong with wanting to change. As an adult, I reached a point when I was confronted head-on with life's demands and my inadequacies. It seemed the world had undone and uprooted me. I had changed. Nevertheless, amid feelings of upheaval, I began to look back on the life from which I had come. I started to peel away the layers, superficially adopted to accommodate to the world around me. In rediscovering my roots, I found that I could work against negative change and begin to transform myself into the person I was *made to be*.

Learning more about our roots inevitably leads to change. The path of rediscovery hinges on a fundamental paradox—to better understand ourselves, we must look beyond ourselves to the lives of those who have gone before us. Our parents, and the generations before them, have left an indelible imprint on who we are. As we fill in, piece by piece, the mystery of our roots—not just *where* we come from but, more importantly, *who* we come from—we will be better able to identify the source of our strengths and how to cultivate those strengths. By the same token, we will be able to understand and improve upon our weaknesses. Perhaps most significantly, we will be able to turn aspects of our past and personality, once construed as weaknesses, into strengths.

It is precisely this counterintuitive kind of thinking that propelled the apostle Paul's outlook on life. Upon his conversion, Paul did a one-hundred-eighty degree turn. He went from persecuting Christians (Phil 3:6) to becoming the foremost advocate of the faith among the early church (and being persecuted himself). As we read in Second Corinthians, amid "weaknesses, insults, hardships, persecutions, and calamities," Paul resolved, "for whenever I am weak, then I am strong" (12:10, NRSV). Instead of resigning himself to defeat and lowering his expectations, he chose to see the silver lining. Paul's weakness became an opportunity for God's power to shine through him.

Change may mean modifying a lifestyle choice to which we previously gave little thought. It may imply a simple shift in referent, like looking anew at a perceived weakness and learning to turn it into a strength. We can be confident that when we make life changes in step with God's purpose, allowing his power to work through us, it always turns out for our good (Rom 8:28).

A MIDDAY RIPOSA

I have worked a couple of nine-to-five jobs in my lifetime. While I did okay at these, I would not say that I flourished. I always put forth my best effort. That's just how I was brought up. The encouraging words of my mom linger with me to this day, who often reminded me, "Whatever you do, work at it with all your heart, as working for the Lord" (Col 3:23, NIV). So I carried on strong throughout the day.

Some jobs afford an ample afternoon break. But most nine-to-five jobs leave just enough time to eat while finishing a segment of a radio or TV program. I find I am at my best when I take a two-hour (or so) respite midday, much after the fashion of the *siesta*—practiced in many European, Latin American, and some Asian countries. In Italian, the siesta tradition is known as the *riposa*. In Italy, all shops, restaurants, churches, and museums close in the afternoon for about two hours. While the timing varies by location, the *riposa* generally corresponds with lunch, beginning anywhere from noon to two o'clock. As a result, the business day stretches beyond the five o'clock closeout those in the States have grown accustomed to. In many places, the norm is a workday that ends at seven o'clock. Most Italians don't start dinner until after eight.

The siesta tradition accommodates those living in warmer climates, whereby they can wait out the most uncomfortable hours of the day. In regions of the world where the siesta is practiced, it is a way of life, reflecting how society is structured.[1] It is not that Italians and the like are weak, running out of gusto sooner than those, for example, of the North American workforce. It's just that Italian customs are arranged differently for various reasons. For the most part, those who observe a siesta work no less than

---

1. Bramblett, "Open Hours in Italy."

those working a straight nine-to-five. Italian society needs just as many hours of labor as any other to meet production needs and keep its markets competitive.

I consider myself blessed that my better half is of French bloodline. My wife spent six years of her early life in France and speaks the language fluently. Since we have been married, some twelve years now, she has always prioritized an afternoon siesta. In France, workers are generally given a one-to-two-hour lunch break.[2] For my wife, a reading interventionist, her day wraps up by mid-afternoon. She's able to enjoy her siesta when she comes home. She also starts fresh at about seven o'clock in the morning and, occasionally, has afternoon or evening responsibilities. My wife works as hard as anyone I know.

Somewhere along the way, having been raised and attended college in the States, I began thinking I did not need or was too good for a siesta. I came to view breaking for a nap at midday as a sign of weakness. By virtue of acculturation, I had developed the mindset that I needed seven to nine hours of sleep each night and, when the day came, was supposed to plow on through. If I found myself dosing off during the afternoon, I did everything in my power to resist the allure. When fatigue got the better of me, and I slipped into a slumber, I was forced to reconcile lingering feelings of guilt. Fortunately, my wife's habits (or, should I say, good graces) have worn off on me over the years. By her benevolent influence and the determined study of my ancestral roots, I gradually conceded to an afternoon *riposa* and, indubitably, have been the better for it.

Studies show that an afternoon siesta is a healthy habit regardless of where we come from. Taking a *riposa* midday is associated with reduced blood pressure, a lower incidence of heart disease, a decreased risk for brain aneurysms, less daytime sleepiness, and an increase in general performance.[3] If we forego that afternoon respite, we could be depriving ourselves of something that would give us an edge up healthwise. For someone like myself, whose ancestry derives from a region of the world where the siesta is observed, shortchanging myself of a midday break runs counter to my makeup. The sleep culture of the United States, where only about a third of adults take a nap, reinforces potentially detrimental neglect of a healthful tradition.[4]

---

2. D. Wright, "Longest Lunch Breaks."

3. Cai et al., "Siesta," 216–18; Brindle and Conklin, "Daytime Sleep," 111–14; Kang et al., "Siesta Habit"; Paraskakis et al., "Siesta and Sleep Patterns," 690–93.

4. Taylor, "Nap Time."

Some people, and many well-meaning Italian Americans I know, trek on through a nine-to-five workday and do fine with the typical half-hour to hour break in the afternoon. They have acculturated. Yet, for many, I surmise, doing so comes not without some inner tumult, having had to set aside an ingrained custom. On the other hand, I (and partly because my work as a professor permits flexibility with my afternoon schedule) have embraced the siesta tradition. The traditional two-hour siesta remains the norm for Mediterranean countries, Latin America, and mainland China (where it is known as the *wujiao*).[5] It stands to reason immigrants from such regions will fare better in US work settings that permit something close to the respite enjoyed in the old country. By way of compromise, perhaps a national initiative allotting at least a sixty-minute lunch break would serve Americans' best interest.

Factors such as the line of work we are in, other responsibilities, how we were raised, and even our personality each influence what our midday break looks like. Occasionally, life gets so busy that we find ourselves eating on the go (or missing lunch entirely). Nevertheless, there are ostensible benefits for incorporating some pause into our daily routine.

LEARNING FROM OUR FOREBEARS

Presently, my *riposa* consists of enough time to eat, do some light reading, and take a nap or go for a walk. Responsibilities inevitably arise, and I have to cut the break short: I am slated to teach an afternoon class or need to pick my kids up early from school. Such is American life. When I am able, pausing from the grind for a siesta helps me stay more attentive and productive in later hours of the day. I typically work into the evening with another break for dinner and family time before the kids go to bed, returning to my office once again at night to write. I sleep less at night than I used to (rarely more than six hours), so it evens out in the end. This schedule suits me. Reintegrating this ancestral tradition has made me more productive.

Some struggle to unearth redeeming values about their ancestors. Society has painted caricatures about the people we come from, leaving us ashamed about our heritage. For others, our upbringing is shrouded in pain, obscuring the image we have of our forebears, and so we'd rather leave the past where it is. Before deciding on the path of willful avoidance, consider that the mores of our ancestors, even if their ways are less than admirable, may hold significance for our life today. At the very least, reconsidering our

---

5. Cai et al., "Siesta," 216.

roots offers an opportunity to learn how we can improve on the ways of those who have gone before us.

In reappropriating the siesta, an ancestral custom, I better understand why I feel and function the way I do. I have learned from inherited mores and adjusted my lifestyle accordingly. Moreover, I have made the most out of something I once viewed as a weakness. Rather than chastising myself for cowering to an afternoon nap, I am intentional about my *riposa*, harnessing an old-world custom to better thrive amid everyday American life.

Reflection Questions:

- For what areas of your life (such as family, work, school, and church) might some change be a good idea? In what ways can rediscovering your roots help you incorporate change in these areas?
- Do you intentionally set aside a break for yourself during the day? If not, what prevents you? While carving out a full two-hour block is unrealistic for many Americans, how could you etch in some additional "me time" to reflect, read, pray, or listen to music. If you're not used to taking a break, start small (even fifteen minutes) and build from there.

4

Where We Come From

and What We're Made Of

Remember the days of old, consider the years long past; ask your father, and he will inform you; your elders, and they will tell you.
—Deuteronomy 32:7, NRSV

Considered the archetype of modern-day pizza, Pizza Margherita was invented in Naples, Italy, in 1889. On the heels of the *Risorgimento* (unification) of northern and southern Italy, the South needed a morale booster to help assuage the loss of their independence. Enter the Queen of Italy, Margherita of Savoy. In celebration of her visit, the famed Neapolitan pizza maker Don Raffaele Esposito prepared a pie with the Queen's favorite ingredients. It just so happened that the ingredients represented the colors of the Italian flag: basil (green), mozzarella cheese (white), and tomatoes (red).[1] Among the numerous varieties of pizza worldwide, Pizza Margherita remains a favorite. The dish's essential ingredients vary little among countries where it is enjoyed; however, its quality and taste differ significantly. If you were to give me a choice between a Pizza Margherita made in the States and one made in Naples, I would go with the Neapolitan pie every time. I have

---

1. Davidson, *Oxford Companion to Food*, 630; Hoffman, *Italy: Little Known Facts*, 10.

been there, tasted it firsthand, and can confirm, indeed—it's fixed with just the right proportion of ingredients and prepared to perfection.

The quality and worth of something are inextricably tied to the place or region from which it originates. If we want to appreciate better what we are made of as a person, we will benefit from learning more about the land and people from which we originated. Founded as a nation of immigrants, most Americans, if they look back far enough, will discover their migrant identity.

WHERE WE COME FROM MATTERS

Consider the commercial slogan for Modelo Especial, "It doesn't matter where you've come from, it matters what you're made of."[2] Without either endorsing or denouncing the product, allow me to elaborate on the meaning behind the slogan. Every time I hear a commercial for Modelo Especial (a beer brand), it arouses my curiosity. Each commercial in the series narrates the success story of a different immigrant, chiefly Latin Americans. The stories themselves inspire. Each raises the Star-Spangled Banner, depicting people from foreign countries, the adversity they have encountered, and the opportunities afforded them in the United States.

One of the Modelo Especial commercials follows the life of Olga Custodio, a Puerto Rican who pursued her dreams of becoming a pilot. While attending college at the University of Puerto Rico, she attempted to enroll in an ROTC program but was rejected because of her sex. Years later, she was accepted into the United States Air Force Officer Training School, en route to making her mark in the history books as the first female Hispanic US military pilot. Custodio served in the Air Force for twenty-four years, earning the rank of lieutenant colonel. After her retirement, she became the first Latina commercial airline captain, flying for American Airlines.[3]

The Modelo commercials deserve credit for championing the accomplishments made by Latin American immigrants. Nevertheless, they inadvertently point to the inopportunity characterizing the migrant's native country. Custodio encountered roadblocks in Puerto Rico yet found open doors in the United States. The first part of the slogan ("it doesn't matter where you come from") incriminatingly represents the migrant's home country. One is left to presume that Puerto Rico offered Custodio very

---

2. Quoted in Peters, "Modelo Is Fighting," under "The ad ('Fighting for Honor with Veteran Juan Rodriguez-Chavez')."
3. Tiscareño-Sato, "Our American Dream."

little—only when she pursued her hopes and dreams elsewhere did her true colors, what she was really "made of," shine through.

Moreover, the product line the commercial series advertises is imported. Modelo Beer "comes from" outside the United States, from a Latin American country, namely Mexico. Although the stories inspire and laud immigrants' indispensable contribution to American society, the commercials mask a double standard. They advertise Modelo as a worthy commodity not because of, but in fact, despite, where it originates. In truth, the United States does not directly contribute anything to its quality. An entirely Mexican product, anything admirable about the beverage, is properly owing to Mexico. It is not my intention to gripe either about the commercial or the merchandise, but simply to point out a false dichotomy—that it is possible to distinguish a product's *origin* from its *quality*. Similarly, it is neither beneficial nor possible to separate the country where someone is born or raised ("where you come from") from a person's worth and character ("what you're made of").

We cannot separate our identity and worth from the place or places our ancestors descended from. If we try to separate *quality* from *origins*, our *character* from our *roots*, or *who we are* (presently) from *where we come from* (in the past), we risk losing touch. Without healthy integration of our present and past experiences—of our self- and ancestral-identity—we are more likely to develop a negative self-image.

RECOVERING OUR ANCESTRAL-IDENTITY

There is a notable correlation between belonging to a *subaltern* (historically marginalized) ethnic group and the likelihood of mental health problems. For example, mood and anxiety disorders are generally more severe among marginalized ethnicities.[4] There is added risk among those from cultural backgrounds that are more *collectivist* (community-oriented). Native peoples and immigrants, for instance, many of whom come from a more collectivist context, may suffer the loss of identity and self-worth in a highly individualized society like America.

For instance, studies have shown an improvement in mental and social functioning among American Indian youth who withstand assimilative pressures.[5] Executive Vice President and Administrative Dean of American Indian College, Joseph Saggio, demonstrates that while the average

---

4. Deaux and Verkuyten, "Social Psychology of Multiculturalism," 132; Settles and Buchanan, "Multiple Groups, Multiple Identities," 165–66.

5. Smokowski et al., "Ethnic Identity," 343–55.

retention rate among national colleges for first-year American Indians is an abysmal 25 percent, schools with an explicit mission to serve Native American students have far greater success. Through positive affirmation and a learner-centric approach, Christian universities such as Bacone College and American Indian College have maintained and even exceeded a critical mass of Native American students.[6] The proactive cultivation of ethnic identity is also linked to improved mental health (moderated anxiety and depressive symptoms) among African, Hispanic, and Asian American young people.[7] Intentionally promoting our ethnic heritage is integral to our overall well-being.

The multicultural makeup of America can make navigating one's roots a challenging exercise. For instance, if someone has each a little Irish, Polish, Ethiopian, and Iranian in her DNA, putting the pieces of her ancestral-identity together will take some work. In the United States, the black-white racial dichotomy further problematizes the matter. By establishing an inherited identity based purely on blackness or whiteness, we risk overgeneralizing our ancestral origins. If society has already determined where we fall on the black-white spectrum—as if skin color was the most accurate measure of identity—we may start to feel like there is no need to dig any deeper.

Ancestry.com has emerged as one of the leading pop culture phenomena of our day. The genealogy site has helped more than 20 million people uncover their family story while selling over 14 million DNA kits.[8] The information provided by Ancestry draws from a database of names and birth origins, developed continuously with the most recent data. The inflow of data fuels the frenetic search to discover where and who we come from. Although statistical data has its value, the subtleties of place and personality that inherited materials and personal conversations afford can get left by the wayside. Sites like Ancestry have their uses, yet offer the most benefit when employed in conjunction with other more personal avenues.

The study of family origins has never been more imperative than it is for Western society today. Genealogy helps us appreciate our individual successes, alongside those of our forebears. Even for someone like me, for whom there is little question about the broader ethnic group to which I belong, there is value in learning more about the particularities of the land and the people I come from. Italy is a very diverse country, regionally and racially. Italy's prominent North-South divide has led historians and

---

6. Saggio, "Native American Christian," 339–42.
7. Smokowski et al., "Ethnic Identity," 345–46.
8. "Ancestry Breaks November Sales Record."

sociologists to speak of two separate races of the Italian people.⁹ Thus, it behooves even me to take a closer look at my roots.

REDISCOVERING THE WHERE, WHEN, AND WHO OF OUR ROOTS

We have all been asked the question—"Where are you from?" More likely than not, we responded with the name of the city, state, or country in which we were born or raised. Depending on the context and length of time, we might respond with the name of the place we currently live. For others, their answer will include a combination of both. Regardless, *where* someone comes from refers to more than a place.

Where we come from, call home, or presently live is tied to a peculiar set of feelings and emotions. It is with this intangible quality that one identifies. Perhaps this point would be more apparent if the question was reworded as—"Where is home for you?" The language of "home" conjures unmistakable feelings. The answer to this question is not necessarily the place someone was born. Home is more than a place. It is where a person finds comfort and belonging. Invariably, home is tied to the people (parents, husband/wife, children, or friends) around whom one experiences that sense of comfort and belonging. I have lived in Hampton, Virginia, for nearly fifteen years. When traveling out of state for conferences, my answer is, "I'm from Hampton." When I convey to my students locally where I am from, my answer is more nuanced. I describe where I currently live and often elaborate where I was raised, "Syracuse, New York." So generally, I find myself still referring to Syracuse as my hometown. It's where I was born—the land of my roots. I spent more years in Syracuse than anywhere else. Alongside where I presently live, Syracuse resonates with me at an emotional, even soulular, level. An integral piece of me is wrapped up in both cities.

Once people identify the *where* of their origins, if pressed further, they inevitably confront the question of *when*: "In what year were you born? In what month?" Or, "What is your astrological sign?" If pressed further still, one runs into questions about family dynamics, such as: "Do you have any siblings? How many? Are you the youngest or oldest?" The answers to these questions lead to queries about one's parents: for example, if someone is an only child, "Is it because your parents came from large families?" If someone has several siblings, it might be assumed that their parents came from smaller families or suffered the loss of close relatives along the way. Thus,

9. Guglielmo, *White on Arrival*, 23–26.

the questions of *where* and *when* are always tied to the more fundamental question of *who*. The line of inquiry invariably shifts to those influences shaping the people who, in turn, have helped shape our own life.

I am from a family of six. My parents decided to have four children, more than the average American family. My folks both came from families of four—closer to the national average at that time of 3.17 persons (based on data collected for 1990).[10] My mom, the elder sibling to one brother, lost her mother and later her brother to illness. Just as her brother was leaving the world, I entered it and inherited his first name, Joseph, as my middle name (Mom has told me more times than I can remember how much my personality is like his). With the means to have more kids, my parents tacked on two more after me. Coming from comparatively smaller families and, for my mom, having suffered the tragic loss of two loved ones, my folks were eager to enlarge the family. Through my siblings and me, they've subsequently had the joy of welcoming eight grandchildren into the world.

If you are like me, you have more than once found yourself in a conversation with an elder loved one about the places and circumstances of the "good ole days." These are often one-ended monologues with which our grandparents, great-grandparents, aunts, and uncles endearingly enchant us. We immensely benefit when we pause and give loved ones an extra moment of our time to listen to their origin stories. Perhaps you have been moved to pen down the details of a family member's past, which unvaryingly becomes the details of your past.

If we have lingering questions about our identity—our personality traits, behaviors, likes and dislikes—then there's no time better spent than sharing stories with family at the table or while sipping a cup of joe on the porch out back on a mild day. Perhaps we persistently lack a sense of inner peace. Maybe we have lurking anxieties about questions of life and death. Many such concerns can be alleviated or resolved through simple conversations with loved ones who lived a generation or more before our own. Our elders are a storehouse of insight and wisdom, waiting to be unlocked. Our parents, grandparents, aunts, and uncles offer a window, not only into our family history but perhaps into God's heart and plans for us. A great conversation starter is to simply ask a loved one where they were born or grew up? More likely than not, they will relish the opportunity to share a bit of their story with you. When we broach our loved one about the *where* question, we inevitably open up new avenues to explore the *when* and, more significantly, the *who* of our roots.

---

10. US Census Bureau, *Abstract of the United States: 1991*, 45.

Reflection Questions:

- Identify some of your foremost character traits (*what you're made of*). How do these traits reflect where you were raised or the places you've lived (*where you come from*)? How do they reflect the land and culture from which your ancestors came?
- What challenges does living in a highly individualized society (like North America and much of Europe) present to our search for self- and ancestral-identity? If your ancestors came from a more collectivist culture, interpret such challenges in light of that background.

PART II

Fostering Our Identity

5

How We Got Here

Rediscovering Our Migrant Identity

Once I thought to write a history of the immigrants in America. Then I discovered that the immigrants were American history.

—Oscar Handlin, *The Uprooted*

WHEN WE REACH BACK, peering through the generations of our family line, we uncover priceless nuggets about who we are and from where we've come. America was built on the strivings and livelihood of immigrants. If Americans gaze far enough into their roots, most will uncover their migrant identity.

My ancestors came to the United States from Italy during the Great Migration beginning in the late nineteenth century. The resources expended by the new Kingdom of Italy left the country in massive debt. Struggling industry, poor living conditions, and oppressive taxation thrust an unprecedented number, some 16 million Italians, from their homeland. The vast majority of these were *contadini* (peasants) from southern regions. As wealthy northerners invested in national securities, the heaviest taxes fell to the southerner. The migrant *contadini* were forced to reconcile their agrarian ways with the urban industrial milieu of America.[1] The Great

---

[1] Zucchi, *Italians in Toronto*, 13–14; D. M. Smith, *Modern Italy*, 211; Brown, "Religion," 538; Nelli, *Italians in Chicago*, 5–6.

Migration encompassed the generation of my great-grandparents. It was chiefly this generation who, as natives of Italy, pioneered the New World on behalf of subsequent groups.

Encompassing either the current or a previous generation, every family has a "migrant" story filled with grim challenges and surprising successes. For example, unless one has Native American descent, families living in the United States likely migrated to the country during the last five centuries.

On the heels of Columbus's inaugural voyage to the Americas in 1492, scores of Spanish explorers settled on what became the continental United States. As Spanish immigrants inhabited the land from Florida to the Southwest, the first French settlers came to the northern regions as traders by the end of the sixteenth century. The advent of European settlement of the New World, reaching into the early seventeenth century, also encompassed the Dutch and English arrival. Africans arrived in large numbers in the seventeenth century, first as indentured servants and then under the slave trade. With the eighteenth century came waves of German migrants, and during the first half of the nineteenth century, the first significant wave of Irish.[2] In the Great Wave of immigration during the late nineteenth and early twentieth centuries, Italians came in droves, alongside Eastern European Jews and newcomers from Greece, Poland, Sweden, Russia, and the Austro-Hungarian Empire (along with teems of more Brits, Germans, and Irish).[3] The twentieth century opened the gates of immigration to Puerto Ricans and Cubans, among others, from the Americas. With the Immigration Act of 1965, the doors to the Eastern Hemisphere opened to the wave of Asian migrants from China, the Philippines, Korea, India, Vietnam, and Japan.[4]

Among the scores of ethnic groups arriving during the Great Wave of immigration, the story of my great-grandparents is too compelling to go left untold. In this chapter, I provide a history of my great-grandparents' pilgrimage to the New World (including a photo assemblage at the end). Their story has helped me appreciate my migrant identity and supplies an example of how rediscovering our roots lends meaning to our lives. Looking afresh at our forebears' challenges and successes empowers us to see our lives as part of a much grander narrative.

---

2. Spickard, *Almost All Aliens*, 36–40; Dinnerstein, *Ethnic Americans*, chap. 1.
3. Spickard, *Almost All Aliens*, 176–207.
4. Spickard, *Almost All Aliens*, 346, 376; Keys, "Immigration Act of 1965," 315–16.

LOOKING BACK TO LOOK AHEAD

As we unearth our ancestral history, we invariably discover more about ourselves. Our forebears' lives integrally inform how we see the world, offering new bearing as we move forward on life's journey. I am grateful to my paternal grandfather, Alfred, and my maternal great-uncle, Dominick, for providing much of the written source material about our family history. Conversations and interviews with family members afforded corroborating details and piquant insights as I charted this history.

Paternal Ancestry

My Dad's Dad's Side

Michele Palma was born in the southern Italian village of Torremaggiore, Puglia, on October 10, 1884. Torremaggiore, a large agricultural center, was prone to drought and economically unstable. Michele, the third of four sons, born to Leonardo Palma and Maria Eccellente, was orphaned at ten. In grade school, Michele accumulated some finances in the art program as an apprentice. From an early age, he and his brothers were artistically talented. Their musical prowess paved the way for the family to reach the New World and make a fresh start. Michele's eldest brother, Domenico, was first trumpet for the San Carlo Opera in Naples, Italy. Silvio, the second eldest, played percussion for the Boston Symphony. The youngest, Anacleto, was a professor of the oboe and member of the Illinois Symphony.[5]

Although musically talented himself, Michele directed his efforts towards developing his trade as a mosaicist. Having saved up enough funds, Michele emigrated to America at the age of twenty-five, joining two of his brothers in Chicago. There he landed a position with the Marshall Field and Company (now Macy's) as an interior decorator. After only a few months in America, Michele underwent a religious conversion from the Catholicism of his youth. This life-altering experience transpired as the fruit of an exchange with Pentecostal church pioneer and father of his future daughter-in-law, Massimiliano Tosetto. The two were working together as colleagues at Marshall Field when Tosetto shared his testimony. In a biographical account of Michele, his son Alfred writes, "my father literally felt the hand of God reach down and pull him by the jacket toward Himself."

Michele was baptized by the Italian evangelist Giuseppe Beretta. While continuing his trade as a mosaicist, he was ordained as a deacon. Michele

---

5. A. Palma, "Michael Palma," 34.

joined a mission on Chicago's West Grand Avenue named the Assemblea Cristiana (Christian Assembly), the first Italian Pentecostal congregation on record. He married the love of his life, Catherina Gardella, on November 19, 1910. Just after WWI, in the deadliest pandemic of the Spanish flu, Michele fell ill. Lying on his sickbed at the point of death, he "covenanted with the Lord, that if he would heal him and raise him up he would go wherever the Lord would send him." Michele eventually recovered. He left for Syracuse, New York, in 1920 with his mother, wife, and children to pastor First Christian Assembly, where he remained for thirty-eight years.[6]

Catherina was born in New York City on February 24, 1885. She was the second eldest of ten children born to Paolo Carlo and Rosa Anna Lidia Gardella, emigrants from Genova, Liguria, Italy, who arrived in the United States in 1880.[7] The family moved to Chicago, where Paolo found work as a waiter. Of Waldensian background, the family joined the First Italian Presbyterian Church of Chicago. Due to disagreement over the Presbyterian mode of baptism (by sprinkling), among other membership requirements, the Gardellas seceded from the Presbyterian Church. They joined a group of independent Italian evangelicals meeting at 1139 W. Grand Avenue. This congregation would become the nucleus of the Assemblea Cristiana. On Labor Day, 1901, Catherina was baptized in Lake Michigan along with eighteen other Italian immigrants.[8]

The mutual tie of the Assemblea Cristiana facilitated Catherina's initial contact with Michele. Together with her husband, she stood among the founders of the flagship Italian Pentecostal denomination, the Christian Church of North America. She was elected as the first Secretary-Treasurer at the denomination's inaugural convention in 1927, a post she held for fifteen years. An accomplished musician, Catherina tendered her piano playing talents to the church. Together with Michele and Massimiliano (her soon to be brother-in-law), she helped compile the Italian Pentecostal hymnal, *Nuovo libro d'inni e salmi spirituali* [New Book of Hymns and Spiritual Songs]. The hymnal's final edition (1959) contained 355 hymns.[9] Fluent in English and Italian, Catherina served through her knowledge of both languages as a counselor and advisor for new believers. She and Michele had eight children—Leah Lydia, Alfred, Edward, Eugene, Leonard, Lydia, Paul, and Helen—several of whom would have a distinguished impact on the transatlantic Italian Pentecostal movement. Catherina died on March 8, 1958, followed by

---

6. A. Palma, "Michael Palma," 34.
7 Ancestry.com, *1900 United States Federal Census*.
8. A. Palma, "A Cloud of Witnesses," 35.
9. Palma and Palma, *Nuovo libro d'inni*.

Michele on October 10, 1963. The two are buried alongside one another in White Chapel Memory Gardens, DeWitt, New York.[10]

My Dad's Mom's Side

Massimiliano Tosetto was born on May 14, 1877, in the village of Campiglia dei Berici, a small agricultural center in the Veneto region of Italy, the son of Luigi Tosetto and Maria Viola. He was raised a devout Roman Catholic. From an early age, Massimiliano proved dedicated to his family, church, and education. At the age of eighteen, his mother's untimely death prompted him to set out on his own. Despite growing up in a town where 80 percent of the population was illiterate, he heeded the recommendation of a former teacher and entered the study of Decorative Art at the Art Institute of Milan.[11]

Massimiliano underwent a religious conversion at the age of twenty-two. As his wife, Maria, tells the story, he was working on a painting project in Milan when he realized it had been an entire year since he last confessed. Massimiliano put together a lengthy list of misdeeds from the prior year and brought it to one of the family parish priests. The priest took one look at it and ushered him along to the next confessional, insisting the list would take too long to work through. He spoke with two more priests, each urging Massimiliano to take his confession elsewhere. Disillusioned by the repeated rejections, he decided it was time to leave the Catholic Church for good. Before he walked away, he requested a Bible from one of the priests, hoping to learn the faith on his own. You might expect the priest would have said no, as reading Scripture among the laity was forbidden in those days. Nevertheless, the priest obliged, though, with the caveat that Massimiliano accept the Bible at a high cost. Massimiliano declined the priest's offer. He continued searching for a Bible and was finally offered one for pocket change by a local Baptist church member, who invited Massimiliano to join him at his congregation. This encounter was the beginning of a new faith journey, inspiring in him newfound freedom to read and interpret God's word on his own accord.[12]

His quest for economic opportunity and the ideal of social and religious liberty drove Massimiliano to the New World. He emigrated and arrived in New York in 1901, finding work as an artisan before transferring to Chicago in 1903. Impressed with his prowess as a fresco painter and

---

10. Find a Grave, s.v. "Rev. Michael Palma"; Find a Grave, s.v. "Kathryn M. Gardella Palma."

11. A. Palma, "Maximillian Tosetto," 1; Toppi, *Massimiliano Tosetto*, 9.

12. Tosetto, interview by Peter Vodola (Maria's grandson).

interior decorator, the Marshall Field and Company hired him on the spot. At a meeting with the evangelist R. A. Torrey, pastor of Chicago's prodigious Moody Church, Massimiliano learned of the "baptism in the Spirit." In 1909, he joined the Pentecostal Assemblea Cristiana. On July 13, 1914, he married Maria Pontarelli. Two years later, he was healed of an ear infection. As Maria describes:

> Brother Tosetto was suffering from a serious ear infection. He took his affliction to the Lord, making this promise—that if he was healed he would be willing to give up his secular labors as an artist and go wherever the Lord would have him, in the field of evangelization. His deliverance was not long in coming. Immediately upon his healing he dropped his secular connections and leaving his family in Chicago, Illinois, he departed for Niagara Falls, New York by the leading of the Holy Spirit.[13]

Massimiliano gave up his profession as a decorator, committing himself to the ministry full-time.[14]

Maria Pontarelli was born in Chicago on December 8, 1891, the fourth of five girls. Her parents, Vincenzo Pontarelli and Philomena Pitassi, had migrated from San Vincenzo, Abruzzi, some years earlier. Raised a devout Roman Catholic, at an early age, Maria was taught to refrain from reading the Bible. Her father made a living as an ice cream vendor, traveling from curb to curb via a mobile cart led by a horse. He set up his shop-on-wheels outside of schools and factories. Maria and her sisters looked forward to leftover cones and sundaes at night. As attending school was not mandatory in early twentieth-century Chicago, to help her family make ends meet, Maria found a job filling and labeling medicine bottles for three dollars-a-week. Her sisters worked in a pecan factory, breaking and sorting nuts. Every penny of the earnings went to help the family with the necessities of food and shelter.

One day, a traveling evangelist left a Bible in the Pontarelli home. First her parents, then Maria, reticently picked up and began reading the story of Jesus in the Gospels. Driven by curiosity, the family visited the Assemblea Cristiana in 1911. While surprised by the boisterous Pentecostal worship, they were captivated by the congregation's sincerity. Maria describes her initial experience at the Italian mission:

---

13. A. Palma, "Maximillian Tosetto," 2.
14. See also my article "Maximillian Tosetto," 2318–19.

> The mission was packed, about 200 people were there worshipping the Lord. My first impressions were naturally impressions of wonder and not a little of fear too. It was difficult to concentrate on meditation. It was noisy with a continued undertone of praise and thankfulness that was difficult for me to comprehend at the time. Services were held each night in the week and three times on Sunday... There were those who always remained after the services to tarry for the infilling of the Holy Spirit. I attended the services every night of the week.[15]

The family would later undergo a religious conversion from Catholicism. With what little they had, her parents bought Maria a pump organ. She committed herself to learning to play it, working studiously through the Italian hymnbook. She learned quickly and used her talents on the organ to serve God.

Massimiliano and Maria founded churches throughout New York and in Massimiliano's hometown, Campiglia dei Berici. For many years, the couple pastored a large church in Niagara Falls. Together, they had five children: Lois, Lydia, Ulda, Esther, and Endor.[16] On August 26, 1944, their youngest daughter, Esther, married Alfred, the second eldest of Catherina and Michele Palma's children. Massimiliano passed away on September 10, 1949, on a preaching mission in Montreal, Quebec. His last sermon, delivered the morning of the day he died, was themed, "Precious in the Sight of the Lord is the Death of His Saints." The message concluded with an exhortation to live in peace and love and with the words, "I feel as though I have wings, ready to fly."[17] He returned to Niagara Falls to be buried by the church "founded and loved by him."[18] Maria died on November 9, 1986. The two are buried alongside one another in Niagara Falls Memorial Park, New York.[19]

---

15. De Caro, *Our Heritage*, 40.

16. Information on Massimiliano's parents and siblings is corroborated by a correspondence from my grandmother, Esther Palma (letter to Lorenzo Quaglio, July 25, 1997).

17. A. Palma, "Maximillian Tosetto," 3.

18. K. Palma, "Final Tribute," 6.

19. Find a Grave, s.v. "Mary Tosetto."

Maternal Ancestry

My Mom's Dad's Side

Angelo Rubbo was born on May 8, 1894, in the village of Pietraroia of the mountainous province of Benevento, Campania, the youngest of two children to Giuseppe and Maria Giuseppa Cusanelli. Angelo worked the fields from an early age, tending his father's sheep so the family might meet the basic needs of a subsistent lifestyle. He was fortunate to be schooled through the third grade, considered a high level of education at the turn of the twentieth century for a small southern Italian town. The family was devoutly Catholic in a village where the nuns and priests ran the church, educational system, and nearly every other activity. Angelo served as an altar boy. At eighteen, he decided to venture beyond the shepherd's life and leave for the New World. His parents scrounged together what funds they could to cover his voyage. Angelo arrived in New York City in 1912, settling among other immigrants from Benevento. In 1917, he joined the US Army. He was honorably discharged a year later due to injury.[20]

On a return trip to Pietraroia in 1919, Angelo married a childhood friend, Carmela Varrone. Carmela (b. June 3, 1899) subsequently joined her husband stateside. The couple moved to Brooklyn, where Angelo landed work as a transit conductor. One day a gentleman on board the train opened the Bible and shared the gospel with him, leading to a religious conversion. Angelo joined an Italian Pentecostal congregation on Brooklyn's Herkimer Street. He and Carmela helped found churches throughout Brooklyn, Queens, and Long Island. The couple had six children: Joseph, Victor, Dominick, Angelina, Elias, and Daniel. Their eldest, Joseph (my grandpa), used to say, "I came over from Italy on the boat." Although he was not born until his parents arrived in the United States in 1920, there's a hint of truth here as Carmela was pregnant with him on her voyage to America. On visits in 1953 and 1954, Angelo and Carmela ministered in their hometown of Pietraroia. Notwithstanding opposition from the local parish priest, the couple founded a chapel next to Carmela's childhood house.[21] Angelo died on May 16, 1955, considerably outlived by Carmela, who passed away on November 13, 1986.[22]

My mom's fondest memory of her grandma is her cooking. Carmela's daily routine included picking fresh fruits and vegetables, meats, and cheese

---

20. Galvano, "Rev. Angelo Rubbo," 36.
21. Galvano, "Italian Christian Church," 37.
22. Ancestry.com, *New York, New York, Death Index, 1949–1965*, s.v. "Angelo Rubbo"; Ancestry.com, *Social Security Death Index, 1935–2014*, s.v. "Carmela Rubbo."

from the local Italian street vendor, preparing all of her food right from scratch. She worked a day job as a seamstress. During dearth economic times, Carmela did everything she could to support her family.

My Mom's Mom's Side

Vincenzo Stigliano (b. September 8, 1878) and Elisabetta DiPizzo (b. December 16, 1889) grew up in the mountainous village of Colobraro in the province of Matera, Basilicata. Vincenzo was born to Giuseppe Stigliano and Maria Rosa Scarpino, one of ten children. Colobraresi homes are built on terraces, one above the other, along a single road that winds around a central peak, Mount Calvario. The family lived in a one-room home with a dirt floor, no furniture, and a mattress filled with corn husks for a bed. Of the ten children, only Vincenzo and an older brother made it to adulthood. Dire economic conditions forced his mother to work long hours to make ends meet. She found a job in the rigorous work of road construction, and subsequently as a shepherdess. The stress of shepherding led to trying circumstances during birth. One day during pregnancy, Maria was out tending sheep when she started having labor pains. As her grandson Dominick describes:

> She couldn't leave the sheep and she didn't think she'd make it back to town. So she laid down under an olive tree, had her baby, and did everything herself. She cut the umbilical cord and tied it... and then she walked back home with the baby, a distance of one to one and half miles.[23]

Despite her efforts, the child lived only for three months. Such were the times.

Vincenzo's father bought him six sheep for his sixth birthday, entrusting him with the responsibility of looking after them. He carried out his shepherding duties by day while attending school at night. At eighteen, he was summoned into military service—a debt all men of age in Italy are expected to fulfill, even to this day. During the reign of Victor Emmanuel II, young men were forced into four years of military service, an improvement from decades earlier when, under Napoleonic rule (1805–14), young men faced up to a seven-year enlistment (today the standard is two years).[24] Many became priests or joined the monastery to evade military

---

23. D. Stigliano, *Stigliano Story*, 13–14.
24. Simon and Abdel-Moneim, *Handbook of Military Conscription*, 15, 84; "Conscription in the Kingdom of Italy."

conscription. With widening emigration channels in the late nineteenth century, men increasingly left for countries abroad to avoid service. Forced conscription was one of the chief reasons Vincezo's older brother, Maurizio, came to America. In a twist of fate, Vincenzo, relatively thin in stature, failed to meet the minimum chest size requirement and was rejected by the Italian military two years in a row.[25]

Vincenzo was just twenty-two when his father passed away from a heart condition. He decided to leave his duties as a shepherd and set sail for America. Vincenzo departed in the hope of making a living in the New World, and with the promise to his mother, who feared losing another child, he would soon return. Vincenzo arrived in New York City in 1902, joining his older brother in Sharpsville, Pennsylvania, where he landed work with a furnace company. When the company shut down three years later, he returned to Italy, yet not empty-handed, having earned a decent sum that he gave, unhesitatingly, to his mother.

Vincenzo decided the time was nigh to get married. In those days, in southern Italy, the parents of the groom customarily arranged the marriage. Having lost his father and not wanting to burden his mother with the task, Vincenzo set out in search of a wife, venturing to the village site he was most likely to meet someone—a *festa*. In the peasantry's folk tradition, *feste* (festivals held on behalf of patron saints) occupy the center of village social life.[26] While there, one Elisabetta DiPizzo caught his eye.

Elisabetta was the youngest daughter of Antonio DiPizzo and Raffaela Capitolo. When Vincenzo entered her life, she was taking extra classes to become a teacher, pursuing a higher level of education than customary in those days. Having cleared permission with Elisabetta's parents, Vincenzo began dating her, and on February 11, 1906, after only a six-month courtship, the two were married. Accompanied by her family and guests, the wedding procession commenced with a walk from Elisabetta's home to the village church to meet the groom and his family. Together with Vincenzo's mother, the newlyweds moved into a house willed to him by his father. Over the next few years, the family faced a severe drought followed by a series of vicious storms. Their crop yield waned, plunging them into debt. In 1911, with Elisabetta remaining in Colobraro to work the farm, Vincenzo returned to the United States.[27]

After a few years apart, Vincenzo decided he wanted the entire family to join him in America. He and Elisabetta had put enough away to purchase

---

25. D. Stigliano, *Stigliano Story*, 38–39.
26. Vecoli, "Prelates and Peasants," 228–33.
27. Douglas Davis, e-mail message to author, August 8, 2020.

the family's emigration papers. However, much of their savings were lost one unfortunate day. Despite strong ties among immediate family, southern Italians are wise to be cautious of extended family. Most peasants live a secluded life in a given landlord's service and thus have little time to forge ties with other village members, including the extended family of aunts, uncles, and cousins. In his *Proverbi Siciliani* [Sicilian Proverbs], folklorist Giuseppe Pitrè cautions the southerner, *cu' havi parenti, havi tormenti* ("who has relatives, has troubles").[28] Elisabetta learned the hard way. She sent a cousin into town with the family's savings to pick up their emigration papers, and the cousin never returned. On top of the resulting financial burden, World War I complicated emigration efforts. Vincenzo's application for American citizenship and his passport expired with the onset of the war. It was another three years before acquiring the requisite documents and legal papers for the family's visas.

After nine years, with financial resources regained and written permissions in hand, Vincenzo's family proceeded with the mandatory emigration physical and vaccinations. Through decrepit onboard conditions and much seasickness in the passage over, the family arrived in New York Harbor in 1921 to behold with great joy the city skyline and Lady Liberty.[29] Vincenzo and Elisabetta had eleven children, with just six making it to adulthood: Mary, Rita, Dominick, Theresa, Esther, and Sarah. Several of their children went on to have prominent ministries in the American Pentecostal church.[30] One can only wonder how many they would have had if not for those nine years apart. Still practicing Catholics at the time, birth control was forbidden.

Vincenzo (d. 1973) and Elisabetta (d. 1980) are buried alongside one another in America's Cemetery, Pennsylvania.[31] Meeting by way of the Pentecostal church network, their daughter, Theresa, married Joseph Rubbo on June 17, 1947. The eldest of Theresa and Joseph's children, Joy (my mom), wed the youngest of Esther and Alfred Palma, Timothy (my dad), on June 10, 1972.

---

28. Pitrè, *Proverbi Siciliani*, 219.

29. Ancestry.com, *New York, Passenger and Crew Lists (including Castle Garden and Ellis Island), 1820–1957*.

30. E. Stigliano (daughter of Vincenzo and Elisabetta Stigliano), interview with the author.

31. Find a Grave, s.v. "James Stigliano"; Find a Grave, s.v. "Elizabeth Stigliano."

PART OF A GRANDER NARRATIVE

Tracing and writing our family history opens a vital window into who we were *made to be*. By digging deeper into my roots, I have discovered I am not just a full-blooded Italian but, despite appearances, am chiefly of southern Italian descent. I have also learned my origins derive primarily from the lower-class peasantry. Even the few ancestors I have from northern Italy were from agrarian villages and meager circumstances. I am grateful I have the opportunity to forge ties with extended family so that, unlike the southern peasant, I can count on them in times of need. Moreover, I've learned the undeniable role of the Pentecostal church in bringing my family together.

In a world preoccupied with the trivial—the box score for last night's ball game, whether another Hollywood couple has broken up, or whether black or grey goes better with our new tie—peering deeper into our roots furnishes a crucial sense of meaning and belongingness. Rediscovering our roots solidifies a more robust understanding of who we are, assuring us that we are part of a much grander narrative. Unraveling the *whos*, *wheres*, and *whens* of our ancestry circumscribes our own identity while impressing upon us the sense that we are part of something significantly greater than ourselves.

Reflection Questions:

- Can you identify the regions of the world (cities, states, countries) from which your ancestors came? How might the particular circumstances they faced in these places have shaped their identity? (You don't have to know the place of origin for every ancestor, but flesh out what you can.)
- Have you unearthed your "migrant identity"? When did your ancestors first arrive to the country? If you haven't started already, I invite you to begin tracing your family history and filling-in your family tree, following the *where*, *when*, and *who* questions as outlined in Appendix A (see my paternal and maternal family trees, Appendix B, for an example).

Plate 5.1. Michele and Catherina Palma, Niagara Falls, New York, 1952. Taken at the 19th Street Church parsonage of their son Alfred. Michele delivered the sermon that Sunday as a visiting minister.
Source: Photo courtesy of Joy Palma.

Plate 5.2. Massimiliano and Maria Tosetto, Niagara Falls, New York, 1947.
At their home on 724 20th Street.
Source: Photo courtesy of Joy Palma.

Plate 5.3. Angelo and Carmela Rubbo, Pietraroia, Campania, Italy, October 2, 1919. Taken on their wedding day, three months before they emigrated for America.
Source: Photo courtesy of Joy Palma.

Plate 5.4. Vincenzo and Elisabetta Stigliano, Villa Nova Restaurant, Sharon, Pennsylvania, February 11, 1956. In honor of their fiftieth wedding anniversary.
Source: Photo courtesy of Joy Palma.

6

Not Just Another Rags to Riches Story

Ethnic Identity and Social Class

Do to others as you would have them do to you.
—Luke 6:31, NRSV

WE'VE COME A LONG WAY

WITH EACH GENERATION OF my family line in America, our economic circumstances improved. As was typical of my ancestors' subsistent lifestyle in Italy, we never had to scrounge for basic needs. The opportunities I enjoy today can be credited to my parents for their faithful day in, day out striving on our behalf, and my grandparents and great-grandparents before them who furnished the foundation for our lives in the New World.

We have come a long way from the one-room tenant homes epitomizing Italian peasant life. It is not uncommon for peasants in Italy's southern regions such as Puglia, Campania, Calabria, and Sicily to sleep on communal beds with several family members. Some share the same room with livestock.[1] I live today in a four-bedroom home with separate

---

1. Tirabassi, "Why Italians Left Italy," 119–20.

bathrooms for kids and parents. When my ancestors embarked on American life, inhabiting the ethnic enclaves of the inner city, they were fortunate to share a single bathroom with the immediate and extended family. The norm was one community wash facility for multiple, even dozens, of families.[2]

Our Sunday dinner tradition played an integral role in shaping our identity as Italian Americans. Everyone at the table could summon their memories, or that of parents and grandparents, of life growing up in Italy. Such familiarity with the old world suggested there was more than an inkling of Italian in my DNA. Yet, there remained a lurking suspicion, sometimes reciprocated in conversations with friends and acquaintances, about my outward appearance: my "light" features don't lend themselves to the stereotypical portrait of the full-blooded Italian. For much of my life, I lived by the assumption that my paternal ancestry traced to northern Italy and that I had inherited my dad's light-featured genes. However, as the family sketch painted in the previous chapter suggests, the majority (six of eight) of my great-grandparents and half of my paternal ancestry hails from the regions of southern Italy. Why then the lighter features? It's hard to say; perhaps there is a recessive gene somewhere in my DNA. Moreover, from my family tree, one can deduce that my ancestry traces mostly, if not entirely, to the *contadini* (the peasant class of farmers and countryfolk).

The *Mezzogiorno* (southern Italy) is steered by a considerable peasant majority, contrasting to the significantly more modern and affluent North. The disparity between the culture of southern and northern Italians has a centuries' long history. The decidedly agrarian landscape of the South, and a feudal system introduced by the Spanish Bourbons in the eighteenth century, produced a society of subsistence-level farm laborers obligated to the owners of large estates.[3] In 1860, led by famed General Giuseppe Garibaldi and his army of a thousand (*Il Mille*), the rising Kingdom of Sardinia conquered the Bourbon controlled South (formerly known as the Kingdom of Two Sicilies).[4] Garibaldi's success precipitated the *Risorgimento* (unification of the country) as the Kingdom of Italy in 1861. After the new Kingdom of Italy defeated Austria in 1866, it liberated and annexed the more privileged northern regions. In the aftermath of the Kingdom's feats, southern Italians became objects of exploitation, taken advantage of by excessive taxes, harsh working conditions, and enforced military conscription.[5] These

---

2. Spickard, *Almost All Aliens*, 187.

3. *Encyclopedia Britannica Online*, s.v. "Mezzogiorno," https://www.britannica.com/place/Mezzogiorno; Tirabassi, "Why Italians Left Italy," 117–18.

4. Doyle, "America's Garibaldi," 69.

5. Fairall, *Italy Struggling into Light*, 634–36; Brown, "Religion," 538.

developments, combined with the late nineteenth-century European agricultural crisis, triggered the Great Migration that brought my ancestors to the New World.

My family derives from the dispossessed southern peasant class, save a couple of artists on my dad's side. And although a step up from the *contadini*, in Italy, artisans remain among the lower classes: below the aristocrats of the top tier and clerics, military, professionals, and intellectuals of the middle class.[6] In building my family history, I have learned that each ancestor on both sides of my family, including the artisans, came from agrarian village contexts. The upward strides our family made is owing to their perseverance and the opportunities seized in the New World.

UNEARTHING OUR ORIGIN STORY

Discovering that my roots trace to southern Italy has given me a brand-new perspective. The resonant story of the *contadini* consists of a journey forged through dearth and marginalization. For many, this story follows a "rags to riches" narrative. *Contadini* left Italy with little and, after spending much of their savings on passage to the New World, arrived in America with even less. For those able to make a living in the United States, they found that they could earn money at a much swifter rate, with an hourly wage surpassing what they would have been privy to elsewhere in Europe or Asia.[7] Peering deeper into my roots has allowed me to identify with and celebrate the trials overcome as well as the immense gains of my migrant forebears.

Nevertheless, my ancestry is significant not merely because I have uncovered this charming rags to riches narrative; its value lies in the story itself. Each person's story has a unique shape. The upper classes of Italy have stories of their own. If we look far enough, we will find that the lives of these peoples, even the royalty, resound with their share of trials overcome and oceans crossed. A palpable sense of identity emerges from the crevices of our present, ordinary experiences when we reach back to unearth the history of the family and loved ones who have gone before us. Harking back to our origins affords added insight into our present circumstances and the social fabric of the world we inhabit today.

The intrigue created by gazing into our roots is the reason why movie franchises have made a fortune on "origin stories." The multiple origin-story series, for example, of the Star Wars and Marvel's X-Men movies, place them

---

6. Gabaccia, *Italy's Many Diasporas*, 39.
7. Spickard, *Almost All Aliens*, 173.

among the top-grossing film franchises of all time.[8] People are intuitively intrigued by origin stories. The history surrounding the people and places of our past and the distant past of our ancestors adds color to and fills in gaps in the present.

REALIZING THE GOLDEN RULE

It is easy to look at others and pass judgment on them because of their social standing. Someone well-off might look at another struggling to make ends meet and write that person off as someone who "reaps what one sows." Someone else might raise an eyebrow at a family from the other side of the tracks, whose house is rotting in mold or property has fallen into foreclosure, pointing to lackluster work ethic or ineptitude as the source for their misfortune. Yet, just as dearth marked my family's first generation in America, a lack of means does not imply a lack of skill or effort.

My ancestors expended nearly all of the resources they had simply to make it to the New World. Upon arrival, they faced job options in industrial America that veered tremendously from the agrarian livelihood that defined their years in Italy's South. Still, they pressed onward. It was not for lack of effort that my great-grandfather Angelo carried on the family work of shepherding. The average sheepherder does not make a significant income, but in the agrarian society where he grew up, this labor was the standard. Sheepherders can make an honest living in America even while standing at the lower end of the economic totem pole. For many laborers like my great-grandfather, their purpose remains an unquestionably noble one. He worked diligently on behalf of his posterity, just as his parents strove tirelessly on his behalf, putting enough earnings away that their son might one day make the journey to the New World.

Similarly, it is easy to sneer at people who live a more privileged life. Someone might belittle the wealth of others, claiming they are overpaid. Even if the case could be made that a given job pays unduly—whither the good in harboring resentment? It is easy to undercut another's success, alleging someone comes from wealth and never had to make the same effort as everyone else. Someone could point the finger at me and say I never had to labor and toil for basic needs; that I was born into a privileged existence. However, in doing so, that person would be overlooking a much grander narrative. While I may have been born into more wealth and opportunity than most, writing off someone's achievements like this overlooks the

---

8. "Franchise Index," Box Office Mojo, https://www.boxofficemojo.com/franchise/?ref_=bo_lnav_hm_shrt.

challenges and toils one's ancestors faced so that subsequent generations could live a better life. Indeed, the success I enjoy today is proportional to the adversity my migrant forebears endured in the early years of my ancestors' experience in America.

Nurturing a deeper appreciation for our ethnic roots helps us look at others' lives with understanding and compassion. It is harder to judge another when we see that person as part of a bigger picture that encompasses the adversity they or their kin may have had to endure. While it is easy to criticize others at face value, taking a moment to consider that our neighbor, like ourselves, is part of a grander story will help us treat that person with the level of understanding we wish others would extend toward us.

Pressing into our roots provides an avenue for upholding perhaps the most foundational and ubiquitous social principle—the Golden Rule. The Golden Rule has been attested to, in some form or another, by most world religions and cultures, reaching back to ancient civilization. The Rule commonly appears in its positive (direct) form, for example, "Treat others as you would like others to treat you." The ancient Greek philosopher Plato referred to the Rule this way, averring: "exactly as we would they should behave to us."[9] The chief New Testament references to the Rule, Matthew 7:12 and Luke 6:31, follow the same pattern: "do to others as you would have them do to you" (NRSV). The principle also appears in the negative form: "do not treat others in ways that you would not like to be treated;" or, as stated by the East Asian philosopher Confucius, "What you do not like if done to yourself, do not do to others." Confucius proceeded to sum up the entire Rule in a single word, "reciprocity."[10] A shortened form also appears in the Jewish Scriptures: "love your neighbor as yourself" (Lev 19:18, NRSV).[11] In Islam, the Rule is stated explicitly in Muhammad's sayings, and implicitly in the Qur'an: "Woe to the defrauders. Those who, when they take a measure from people, they take in full. But when they measure or weigh to others, they cheat" (83:1–3).[12] Formulations resembling the Rule can also be found in Hinduism, Buddhism, Taoism, and Zoroastrianism.[13]

Whether someone is from a Judeo-Christian or Hindu background, is Italian or Chinese, considered rich or poor, or black or white, rediscovering our roots helps us understand and reconcile our differences. By tapping into

---

9. As quoted in Spooner, "Golden Rule," 6:310–11.

10. As quoted in Spooner, "Golden Rule," 6:310–12. See also Flew, *Dictionary of Philosophy*, 125.

11. See also Mark 12:31.

12. Translated by Talal Itani. See also Gensler, *Ethics and the Golden Rule*, 43–44.

13. Kidder, *How Good People*, 159.

a narrative encompassing our ancestors' challenges and successes, we are able to view those from other cultural contexts in light of the larger story informing their walk of life. In doing so, we actualize the goal of "reciprocity."

Reflection Questions:

- What opportunities do you enjoy that perhaps you also take for granted? In what ways did the challenges or successes of your forebears make these opportunities possible?
- Do you ever find yourself quick to judge someone based on his or her apparent social status? How can learning about our roots (and the roots of others) help us treat our neighbor as we would want to be treated, thus better realizing the Golden Rule?

7

Forays into the Problem of Racial Identity

What we need to do is learn to respect and embrace our differences until our differences don't make a difference in how we are treated.
—Yolanda King

I HAVE, ADMITTEDLY, BEEN the object of little racism over the course of my life. I have to think hard to recall an instance when I, a perceptibly white person, was the object of discrimination. Racial identity is a complex subject with crucial implications for understanding ethnicity and our ancestral roots. The narrative of racial discrimination has irrevocably tainted the history of America. Allow me to say upfront that I am in no way immune to this disease. I am culpable for racist thoughts and inclinations. I am convinced that admission of our innate penchant for racism, not just as Americans but as citizens of a fallen world, is paramount to any healthy discussion about race issues.

SOURCES OF RACISM IN ITALY

The story of my ancestors sheds light on the lamentable race narrative of the United States. Like America, the history of Italy is marred by a prominent divide along the lines of race. As explained in the previous chapter, the rift between northern and southern Italians reaches back several centuries. My forebears left Italy when the disparity between northerners and southerners was most pronounced. The North-South distinction remains intact today, accented by a manifest economic divide. The Great Migration period, in the aftermath of Italy's unification efforts, was marked by a definite gap between northern and southern Italians. In subsequent years, this disparity was articulated in terms of two distinct races. However, in America, the most popular transoceanic destination of Italian émigrés, the final step in defining two races of the Italian people came to fruition.[1]

At the turn of the twentieth century, tensions mounted as enclaves of Italians formed in America's urban hubs. Rivalries ensued between burgeoning Italian colonies and longstanding ethnic groups of the early-to-mid-nineteenth-century migrations dominated by northern and western Europeans.[2] For example, Sicilians and Swedes were known for their "bloody battles" using sticks, knives, guns, and blackjacks. Meanwhile, Swedish and Irish youth recurrently engaged in similar skirmishes on playgrounds and streets with their Sicilian counterparts.[3] Despite their common Catholic lineage, the Irish, who emerged by the start of the twentieth century as the dominant ethnic group in American Catholicism, harbored resentment for the Italians.

The most recent chapter in Italian history encompassed the 1870 overthrow of Rome and seizure of the Holy See by the Garibaldi-led forces of the Kingdom of Italy.[4] Although a strategic military move, as the papacy's political power rivaled that of the Kingdom, the Vatican's capture also expressed Garibaldi's anti-Catholic sentiments. Middle- and upper-class Italians fueled intense nationalistic and anti-papal views, leading to the conquest of the Roman See. On the streets of America, northern Italians celebrated the anniversary of Rome's occupation with parades and by erecting statues of the Kingdom's leaders in public parks.[5] A large peasant class, epitomizing southern Italy's socioeconomic makeup, accounted for

---

1. Gabaccia, "Race, Nation, Hyphen," 45.
2. Nelli, *Italians in Chicago*, 8–9.
3. Guglielmo, *White on Arrival*, 25.
4. Fairall, *Italy Struggling into Light*, 784–85.
5. Vecoli, "Prelates and Peasants," 224.

but a fraction (1 percent) of the nationalist movement.[6] Still, the strong Irish American Catholic base presumed all Italians alike were culpable for the atrocity against Rome, vilifying the innocent southerner alongside northerners as "jailers of the Holy Father." One can see why the Irish were more likely than not to greet the Italian newcomers with "brickbats rather than bouquets."[7]

The isolated southern villager was unacquainted with modern notions of radicalism and nationalism. Southern Italians shared neither the same interests nor the allegiance to the Kingdom of Italy that exemplified their northern counterparts.[8] Nevertheless, in the New World, southerners encountered the same disdain as northerners from American Catholics. It is worth noting that Italians, on the whole, were considered more peaceable than other immigrant groups among the polyglot of ethnicities encompassing America's urban centers. Italians, for the better part, avoided friction with other migrant groups like the Jews (with whom they arrived in America at about the same time) and Asians. Furthermore, only rarely did Italians quarrel with other European groups. While hostilities did exist with Swedes and the Irish, immigrants with a reputation for rubbing shoulders with other groups, these occurrences were isolated and only rarely resulted in bloodshed.[9]

The southern Italian's rustic roots clash with the modern, urban-industrial milieu of American society. For the peasant, the process of acculturation is a longer and more strenuous one than for the typical northerner. When conflicts arose in the ghetto with other groups or property value declined, an easy scapegoat for landowners was to point to the Italian peasant. In 1899, the US Bureau of Immigration formally distinguished the northern "Keltic" from the southern "Iberic" Italian.[10] With this move, a geographical North and South of Italy were clearly defined, and subsequent migrants were categorized accordingly upon entry.

Northern and southern Italians were distinguished along physical, mental, and social lines. Southerners were considered shorter in stature and darker by complexion, as suggested by common early twentieth-century racial epithets such as "dark people" and "blackhands."[11] Southern Italians were deemed poorly educated, lacking in initiative, and less apt to make the

6. Gabaccia, *Italy's Many Diasporas*, 39.
7. Vecoli, "Prelates and Peasants," 222.
8. Vecoli, "Prelates and Peasants," 227–28.
9. Sowell, *Ethnic America*, 111.
10. Guglielmo, *White on Arrival*, 23.
11. Guglielmo, *White on Arrival*, 19, 25.

same economic strides as their northern counterparts. For a given migrant, if a southern bloodline was determined, that person was labeled and either refused entry entirely or permitted but with specific provisions in place should they subsequently be associated with social unrest. Thus, the United States provided the formal terminology that would render the Italian people from that point forward into two separate races.

PARALLEL NARRATIVES: RACE IN ITALY AND THE UNITED STATES

But is the United States really to blame for the bifurcation of Italians into their respective northern and southern classifications? Racism in America along the black-white axis has a longstanding history. Arguably the most profound force in shaping and reshaping the country, the black-white divide in America finds a parallel in the North-South distinction among Italians.

The institutions of slavery and segregation came at a steep price. Consider the Civil War cost: 2.4 percent of the American population was lost in the war's bloodshed. For comparison, if the same percentage of America's citizens were killed in a conflict today, the number of casualties would be nearly 7.5 million. One could add to the final tally those killed in the Kansas wars that precipitated the Civil War and lives lost in the paramilitary conflicts in the South during the Reconstruction years. In America, the pursuit of racial equality has come at an immense cost.[12]

The emergence of the "Keltic-Iberic" nomenclature suggests that America perpetuated, if not caused, the decisive division of Italians into two races. Southerners were distinguished from northerners on statistical grounds just as any nationality group is differentiated from another. The new terminology brought into focus and formalized the developing consciousness that Italy was comprised of two separate peoples. It is in this respect that the North-South (Keltic-Iberic) bifurcation reflected, more than affected, the racial profile of the United States. The dehumanizing machinery of racism held intact well after the Thirteenth Amendment abolished slavery in 1865, maintaining a lens through which subsequent immigrant groups would be weighed, classified, and discriminated against. The Great Migration of Italian peasants coincided with the race-specific restrictions of the Black Codes and the Jim Crow Laws of the late nineteenth and twentieth centuries. Under the guise of "separate but equal," US segregation would only legitimize and reinforce the southern Italian's alienation.[13]

12. McPherson, *War That Forged a Nation*, 2, 173.
13. Drescher, *Abolition*, 330–31.

The anti-southern prejudice was epitomized in the lynching of Iberics, with the most infamous account occurring in 1891 at a New Orleans prison. Several Italians were being detained as suspects in the murder of the New Orleans Chief of Police. Although the chief had given no identification of his assailants, he said he was shot by "dagoes" (a disparaging term for someone of Italian, Spanish, or Portuguese descent) before taking his last breath. A jury of twelve announced a verdict of acquittal—the State was unable to convict a single Italian standing trial. Instead of releasing the detainees, the judge remanded them to jail. The following morning, a mob of five thousand rioters met at the city center, among whom could be heard the cry, "Death to the dagoes!" The disgruntled horde marched through the city, making one stop at the Canal Street gun store to load up on rifles and shotguns. Arriving at the prison, the mob trampled the door. About fifty rioters proceeded through the opened corridor. Reportedly, the warden locked up the non-Italian prisoners but left the Italians to fend for themselves. The assailants reached the Italians' cellblock, and when the raid was over, eleven Italians had been murdered.[14]

It stands to reason that the massacre could have been prevented by the New Orleans law enforcement, as the time and place of the mob meeting was publicly announced beforehand in one of the city newspapers.[15] Another publication, *The Annual Register, 1891*, describes the fate endured by one of the prisoners:

> He had already been fatally wounded, and his dark face was besmeared with blood. As the crowd in the square caught sight of him they uttered a roar of rage. They had heard the shots within the jail but had not seen slaughter. Now was their opportunity. Someone brought a rope, which was noosed and thrown around the man's neck. The other end was cast over the limb of a tree. The dying wretch was swung up, then a fusillade from a score of weapons ended his sufferings.[16]

As staggering as the image painted here is, it is consistent with other depictions of lynchings in the American South.[17]

The race problem in America came to be defined by the outlying characteristic of skin color—perhaps the most obvious way to differentiate portions of the world's population. Although a superficial way to categorize

---

14. Musmanno, *Story of the Italians*, 125–29.
15. Musmanno, *Story of the Italians*, 126.
16. Quoted in Musmanno, *Story of the Italians*, 129.
17. For a portrayal of the cruel but unfeigned parallel between lynching and the Cross in African American history, see Cone, *Cross and the Lynching Tree*.

people, skin color serves as a practical indicator of the part of the world to which someone's roots trace. Studies show that peoples living closer to the equator, including much of Africa and Latin America, have darker skin to protect them from the higher exposure to sunlight. On the other hand, those living further from the equator, including much of North America and Scandinavia, adapted by developing paler skin, which better absorbs the muted sunlight characterizing these regions. Anthropologist Nina Jablonski suggests that some African Americans suffer from vitamin D deficiency because of the rupturing way the slave trade had thrust them from their familiar surroundings. African migrants lacked the time needed to acclimate to the scanter amounts of sunlight in North America.[18] So then, skin color has a biological function; nevertheless, this does not justify using the color of one's skin to demarcate a so-called inferior, less-evolved race.

For sociological reasons, some would argue that one portion of society is always the object of marginalization. *Dominant-subaltern* critical theory points to the reality that every social order contains some groups superior to others. However, this theory is not merely descriptive but suggests an innate human propensity by which one ethnic group always elevates itself at another's expense. Historically, the promotion of ethnicity in this way has often been achieved by intentional and forcible means.[19] For example, the paler-skinned peoples of northern and western Europe assumed a dominant position by invoking the color line to exploit the more vulnerable, darker-skinned African peoples. The first phase of this mass subjugation was importing African slave labor by Spain to facilitate their conquest of the Americas. The subsequent epoch of British colonialism in the United States was also characterized by African slave importation. Although the transatlantic slave trade was barred in the wake of the Jefferson administration and British Abolition Bill (1806–7), domestic trading was used in ensuing years to fuel the deep South's cotton plantations.[20]

In Italy, feudalism followed a similar pattern of exploitation. Early twentieth-century Italian philosopher Antonio Gramsci argued that modern Italy's makeup perpetuates the southerner's relegation. Through the cooperative efforts of the dominant classes (the bourgeoisie elite and intellectuals), Gramsci claimed the Italian state facilitated the peasant class's subordination. The language barrier represented their marginalization, with the bourgeoisie and intellectuals speaking Italian and the peasants their local dialects. By ignoring or explaining away peasant arguments for agrarian

---

18. Gibbons, "Shedding Light," 934–36.
19. Harindranath, *Perspectives on Global Cultures*, 51–62.
20. Drescher, *Abolition*, 39–40, 169.

reform, Italian society deprived them of their ability to transform society, promoting their condition of servitude and empowering fascism.[21] Their penurious, agrarian roots distinguish Africans and southern *contadini*. These origins make each more susceptible to coming under the dominion of affluent groups who have a more developed and better endowed social, political, and military structure.

THE STING OF SOCIAL DARWINISM

There are several reasons as to why Africans and the southern *contadini*, among others, became the object of exploitation in America. In addition to their agrarian mores, a notable and far less justifiable reason is social Darwinism, emerging in the mid-nineteenth century. English biologist Charles Darwin articulated a new scientific evolutionism in his 1859 book, *On the Origin of Species*. Darwin mapped his *natural selection* theory in this work, providing the foundation for the "survival of the fittest" principle. Accordingly, among other peoples, Africans were subject to disparagement because they were genetically less fit to succeed.[22] Together with other agrarian migrants, their alleged ineptitude was blamed on their makeup as inferior hominids. Thus, the so-called inability among such groups to excel in America, socially and economically, was explained from the standpoint of genetics, more than the straightforward reason that they were out-of-place agricultural folk who had been thrust into a foreign, industrialized context.

As suggested by the United States' third president and principal author of the Declaration of Independence, Thomas Jefferson, the crisis of cultures the agrarian migrant experienced goes a great distance in explaining their apparent ineptitude and misconduct. In his *Notes on the State of Virginia*, Jefferson wrote:

> That nature has been less bountiful to them in the endowments of the head, I believe that in those of the heart she will be found to have done them justice. That disposition to theft with which they have been branded, must be ascribed to their situation, and not to any depravity of the moral sense. The man, in whose favour no laws of property exist, probably feels himself less bound to respect those made in favour of others. When arguing for ourselves, we lay it down as a fundamental, that laws, to be just, must give a

---

21. Gramsci, *Selections from Cultural Writings*, 206–8.
22. Darwin, *Origin of Species*; Spencer, *Principles of Biology*, 444.

>reciprocation of right: that, without this, they are mere arbitrary rules of conduct, founded in force, and not in conscience.[23]

Jefferson is addressing the perception that some minorities are intellectually inferior and prone to misconduct. For the sake of argument, he concedes the perception, lest his critics miss the more integral point—that the same people demonstrate much heart, an indispensable virtue, and one often lacking among the privileged, majority classes. For Jefferson, it was chiefly their *condition*, rather than their *nature*, that contributed to how ethnic minorities behaved. Based on Jefferson's critique, perhaps the more fitting assessment of Italian slums would be that their circumstances owed principally to their poverty, over against immorality and crime.

Much of the alleged crime among Italians can be attributed to the misunderstandings they experienced as a people immersed in a new environment, with laws and standards suited to the Anglo-Saxon majority. According to Enrico Sartorio's firsthand history of the period, the political administration of turn-of-twentieth-century Italy "practically compelled a man to take the law into his own hands in order to safeguard his interest, his family and his life."[24] In hindsight, Italian Americans committed fewer crimes during the twentieth century than commonly maintained. Moreover, the crimes they were culpable for were usually gambling and fighting, rather than professional criminal activities (such as fraud, burglary, or armed robbery).[25] In his 1880 account of the slum conditions of New York City's lower east side, *How the Other Half Lives*, Jacob August Riis wrote: "The swarthy Italian immigrant has his redeeming traits. He is as honest as he is hot-headed. There are no Italian burglars in the Rogues' Gallery; the ex-brigand toils peacefully with pickaxe and shovel on American ground."[26] Despite their quick temper and occasional skirmishes, Italians earned a reputation for being an honest and hardworking people.

The undercurrents of social Darwinism in the United States manifested in rigorous immigration procedures to ascertain the specific bloodline of new entrants. Italians determined to possess even a trace of African descent were immediately differentiated from their "white" northern counterparts as "dark whites" and thereafter treated as inferior.[27] Studies, based on purportedly scientific findings, maintained that the bloodline of Iberic (southern) Italians traced to the regions of North Africa. Social Darwinism then,

---

23. Jefferson, "Notes," 268–69.
24. Sartorio, *Social and Religious Life*, 24.
25. Sowell, *Ethnic America*, 118.
26. Riis, *How the Other Half Lives*, 47.
27. DeSalvo, "Color: White/Complexion: Dark," 28.

coupled with the criminality of a few—for example, the Sicilian Mafia—precipitated the heightened immigration quotas of the twenties. The United States levied similar sanctions against Latin American immigrants. During the Great Depression, some 500,000 Mexicans were forcibly deported, many of whom were US citizens. Such quotas made it increasingly difficult for large numbers of migrants from one region to enter the country together at the same time and naturalize.[28]

Jews also became objects of discrimination at the hands of the supposedly superior Anglo-Saxon (or Nordic) race. By extending Darwin's evolutionary principles, Francis J. Galton theorized that heredity dictated mental, emotional, and creative qualities in addition to physical traits; thus, providing the substructure of modern-day *eugenics*. Not only did white supremacy in America relegate Jews by restricting employment and educational opportunities, but the practice of Galton's theory—via *negative eugenics*—precipitated the concentration camps of Nazi Germany.[29]

THE MYTH OF RACIAL BLINDNESS

I have not experienced the discrimination characterizing the daily existence of many ethno-racial groups in America. Nor can I say that I have encountered the extreme ostracism and misunderstanding my southern Italian ancestors faced. I offer the above narrative on the history of racism in Italy and America to explore ground for further thinking and conversating about our ethnic roots. I remain aware of (and riddled by) my apparent "whiteness." Upon birth, I indubitably became a "white" citizen (my actual color is more of a beige with pinkish hues). For some inexplicable reason, I inherited my dad's lighter features instead of the stereotypically-Italian, darker traits of my mom (and my sister, who is the spitting image of her).

As soon as someone enters America, either by birth or immigration, he or she is aligned with a predetermined social group based on an outlying, accidental trait—the color of our skin. The color line is polarizing; traditionally, there has been very little "in-betweenness." We are either black or white. The nation's Latina/o population, although many settled in America before the United States became a country, was cast aside during the segregation period because they were neither "black" nor "white." Some were labeled "half-breeds," while many others, including the surge of Puerto Rican farmers in the mid-twentieth century, were exploited for cheap labor

---

28. Gabaccia, "Race, Nation, Hyphen," 55–56; Medina, *Mestizaje*, 4–5.
29. Black, *War Against the Weak*, 13–19.

under poor working conditions.[30] With the 1965 Immigration Act and the replacement of several exclusionary laws, the arrival of a new wave of Asian migrants and their reputed "yellowness" has expanded the referent.[31] As a nation, slowly, Americans are beginning to read between the lines. Although racial "science" labels all Italians as white (or, more precisely, "dark white"), there are, of course, cases where the skin color of an Italian is darker than that, for instance, of an African immigrant. While providing a clue into one's origins, skin color, by itself, can be quite arbitrary as a label.

Perhaps you have heard someone say, either superficially or sincerely, "I don't see color." While the intent behind this claim (which is well and good if meant to convey that one aims not to judge another by their skin color) may be warranted, such a blanket statement strikes me as a bit naive. The person making such a claim risks putting him or herself above racism—an attitude that is precarious and shortsighted. The better approach is to admit that you and I, like everyone else, have a penchant for racism and remain a "work in progress." From here, we can proceed to the healthful acknowledgment of our individual ethnic and racial identity.[32] There is value in appreciating our color and complexion and our tallness or shortness of stature. Our physical traits are part of what makes each of us unique, inviting us to inquire further into the *where* and *who* we have come from.

The host of *The Late Show* on CBS, Steven Colbert, previously aired (as host of Comedy Central's *The Colbert Report*) a segment called "I Don't See Race." The segment's premise is encapsulated in the typical Colbert saying: "I don't see race. People tell me I'm white and I believe them."[33] In this quote, Colbert takes a witty approach to an otherwise delicate topic. The segment proceeds with social commentary that makes light of prominent stereotypes. The show is an example of how *racial blindness* (not acknowledging color or race) has entered the mainstream of American media. The comical manner through which the topic is approached points to the evolution of racism as a whole.

Today, it is less common for Americans to admit that they are racist. During the sixties, at the peak of the Civil Rights movement, it was customary for white people to acknowledge prejudices and racial superiority. As antiracist educator Robin DiAngelo suggests, fewer claiming they are racist does not mean that racism has disappeared. Racism endures

30. Medina, *Mestizaje*, 5. See also Recinos, *Hear the Cry*, 58–59.
31. Keys, "Immigration Act of 1965," 315–16.
32. For an elaboration of the dangers of the "colorblind" mentality, see Mazzocco, *Psychology of Racial Colorblindness*. See also Thandeka's discussion of racial identity in light of the "process of becoming white" (*Learning to Be White*, 86).
33. Quoted in Frieden, "I Don't See Race."

because it is "highly adaptive."[34] People are no longer categorized as rigidly as they were during the Jim Crow era. Today there is more readiness to acknowledge the "grey" area between black and white—the many people of mixed race and the broad spectrum of ethnicities that lie somewhere in between. However, neither admitting our so-called color blindness nor the Civil Rights movement itself signals an end to racism. Indeed, failing to acknowledge race impedes the ability to understand our prejudices. As DiAngelo maintains: "While the idea of color blindness may have started out as a well-intentioned strategy for interrupting racism, in practice, it has served to deny the reality of racism and thus hold it in place."[35] It is much too premature to think that America has turned the corner on racism's systemic implications. While admitting to racial bias may be uncomfortable, we set the clock back on progress when we refuse to acknowledge something that persists.

FINDING EQUALITY AND DIVERSITY IN THE IMAGO DEI

Embracing our roots entails rediscovering who we were *made to be*. Indeed, we were made to reflect the character of God. The pursuit of racial harmony is at the heart of God's redemptive plans for creation. As the Associate Professor of Missions at Regent University, Alemayehu Mekonnen, suggests: "In the pursuit of freedom, equality, and justice, humanity is not alone. The God of the Bible, who is the defender of the poor, the orphans, the widows, the oppressed, and the exploited, has compassionately identified with the destitute and fought for them through his prophets, Jesus Christ, and the apostles."[36] Mekonnen's claim is even more impactful, writing as someone of African origin who, like the Israel of Scripture, lived in exile for many years (more than three decades) because of ethno-racial marginalization. Despite the adversity he encountered in a region for centuries oppressed by Western powers and today exploited by Chinese influences, Mekonnen lauds the God of Scripture as his deliverer.[37] God stands on behalf of African peoples, and others who have suffered discrimination, because freedom and equality are intrinsic to his character.

On the one hand, racial equality means recognizing that something essential unites each one of us. Our equality is rooted in our inherent

34. DiAngelo, *White Fragility*, 40.
35. DiAngelo, *White Fragility*, 42.
36. Mekonnen, *The West and China in Africa*, xvi.
37. Mekonnen, *The West and China in Africa*, 236–37.

dignity as creatures made in the image of God.[38] On the other hand, each of us was made unique. According to Genesis 1:26, human diversity reflects the plurality in God: "Let *us* make humankind in *our* image, according to *our* likeness" (NRSV).[39] The use here of the plural pronouns hints at the Trinity—a reality that is both one in essence (equal) and comprised of unique persons (diverse). Hence, while the issue of racial identity must be approached in light of *equality* (our shared dignity) in God, it must also be considered in view of our unique *diversity* in God.

The passing of the Civil Rights Act of 1964 signified raising the banner of equality in the face of discrimination, segregation, and disenfranchisement.[40] Nevertheless, to effectually uphold the spirit of the civil rights movement, we must also reclaim the value of our differences. We must push past the black-white binary and uncover our rich diversity. We must confront the inherent reductionism of the color line and circumscribe on our consciences how each person is exceedingly more than "black" or "white." Baptist minister and civil rights activist, Jesse Jackson, likens a united America to the panoply of the colors on a rainbow: "We must forgive each other, redeem each other, regroup, and move on. Our flag is red, white and blue, but our nation is a rainbow—red, yellow, brown, black and white—and we're all precious in God's sight."[41] Indeed, America represents a color spectrum that is much more diverse, and when reflecting the light of God's image in harmony and reconciliation, far more beautiful.

Rediscovering our roots allows us to appreciate the ways each one of us is unique. The inimitability of our family tree, tracing to countless persons and places, encompasses our diversity. Building my family history has helped me see beyond my "Americanness," "Europeanness," and "whiteness." Peeling back a layer at a time, I have found that I am not only Italian but that my bloodline traces chiefly to the agrarian folk of southern Italy. Peeling away another layer reveals the multiple regions my ancestry tracks to (Puglia, Abruzzi, Campania, and Basilicata) and, one more layer, to numerous cities and villages. As we unearth the nuances of each village and family name to which our heritage traces, we add a new argument to our behalf, controverting our alleged "whiteness" or "blackness" in favor of our uniquely diverse cultural origins.

There is nothing intrinsically misleading about one's outward appearance (e.g., skin color, stature, or facial features). Our differences reflect

---

38. Murray, *Saving Truth*, 111–12.
39. Emphasis added.
40. Hersch and Shinall, "Fifty Years Later," 425–27.
41. Jackson, "1984 Democratic National Convention," 575.

the diversity embodied in the *imago Dei* and fuel the healthy exploration of our roots. The danger lies in preemptively labeling either ourselves or others. When we do, we risk overlooking the authentic discovery of our roots and, consequently, our unique identity and purpose. It is easy to judge a book by its cover. Labeling someone else or ourselves based on outlying characteristics is an easy trap to slip into. On the other hand, if we "blindly" deny our differences, we are only perpetuating the seeds of racism. The way forward lies in reaching beyond appearances while maintaining a critical stance that acknowledges the depth and complexity of the issue of race. If we want to find out more about *where* and *who* we have come from, we must first admit our present bias. And then we have to do some digging.

Reflection Questions:

- Can you recall a time when you were either the object or initiator of racism? How does admitting our innate penchant for racism inform how we look at such experiences?
- Can you identify an instance when you or someone you know resorted to the supposed ideal of *racial blindness*? Instead of ignoring the reality of racial differences, how can you recognize and affirm someone's ethnicity, culture, or race?

8

On Being a Religious Italian American

but Not a Good Catholic

For if you forgive others their trespasses, your heavenly Father will also forgive you.

—Matthew 6:14, NRSV

MY PARENTS MET IN New York City in 1967 at the annual convention of the Christian Church of North American (CCNA). Teenagers at the time, they had likely seen or run into one another much earlier than that. As the story goes, my folks had been attending the denomination's conventions together with their parents for years, meaning they were likely playmates in the same nursery room as toddlers. The CCNA, our family denomination, was founded as the first nationally-sanctioned body of Italian Pentecostal churches in the world. The distinguished history of Italian Pentecostalism reaches to the 1907 Chicago revival among a band of inner-city migrants, with close ties to the better-known Azusa Street, Los Angeles revival (widely regarded as the birthing ground of worldwide Pentecostalism).[1]

---

1. Robeck, *Azusa Street Mission*, 6–8; R. M. Anderson, *Vision of the Disinherited*, 66, 128–29. The CCNA became the International Fellowship of Christian Assemblies in 2006 (see my book, *Italian American Pentecostalism*, 100).

My family's religious heritage traces deep into the tributaries of the Pentecostal movement. Such a history veers from the stereotypical profile of the "Catholic" Italian. Nevertheless, the influence of Catholic spirituality can be discerned in the fiber of our family's religiosity. Indeed, one's religious identity is inseparably tied to one's ancestral heritage. Even if we move away from our forebears' affiliation, or, abandon organized religion entirely, our heritage leaves an impression on our conception of faith and divine things that is worth returning to.

REVISITING OUR RELIGIOUS HERITAGE

Everyone follows some religion. *The Merriam-Webster Dictionary* defines *religion* as "a cause, principle, or belief held to with ardor and faith."[2] According to this definition, even the atheist is, in some sense, "religious." The atheist upholds a belief system built on faith in a universe originating and sustained by natural processes. From this perspective, it is impossible not to be religious. If identifying with the ways of our ancestors promises to improve our well-being, it behooves us, even the atheist, to examine our religious roots. Even if we are convinced our heritage is useless, there is merit in revisiting our roots as an opportunity to learn more about our inherited beliefs.

Perhaps we have undergone a religious conversion; we still stand to benefit from learning how our new religion lines up with the old. While some hardliners will say a person cannot discover anything from a cultural context outside Western Christianity, I would aver that we can learn from any religious experience if we adopt the right mind frame. Consider someone moving from an East Asian tradition to a mainline Protestant context. Does not this person stand to benefit from harnessing the intrinsically more communal makeup (although rooted in ancient Confucianism) of the East Asian culture?[3]

To continue the above example, it is noteworthy that Confucian thought is known for its emphasis on *filial piety* (respect for our parents, elders, and ancestors). Professor of Theology and Mission at Fuller Seminary, Amos Yong, suggests Western contexts like the United States can glean from Confucian philosophy by critically engaging it. According to Yong, a Malaysian-born Chinese immigrant, the Asian American community, in particular, ought to consider the implications of Confucianism in light of building their homes on the New Testament model of filial respect:

2. *Merriam-Webster Dictionary*, new ed., s.v. "religion."
3. Ketcham, *Individualism and Public Life*, 71–72.

> There are certain biblical themes such as honoring of parents and the submission of women (read off the surface of some Pauline texts) that resonate with the filial piety of especially Confucian cultures, and these have inevitably become central issues for the forging of Asian American identities. Hence Asian American immigrants who are attracted to Christianity are often drawn to evangelical Protestantism because it provides a similarly conservative worldview, one that enables their acculturation into American society.[4]

In understanding the shared ethic of filial piety, in this case, between evangelicalism and Confucianism, one better grasps the nuances of their faith commitment and the sources informing how they see the world. Moreover, it would appear that American Protestants, as they navigate Western culture's *private* and *individualistic* leanings, would do well to consider the Confucian emphasis on the *public* and *collective* dimensions of human life.[5]

Although remaining within the broader Christian tradition, my ancestors converted from the Catholicism of the old-country to American Protestantism. However, they retained, arguably for the better, aspects of their religious heritage. In addition to being a clue into my innate southern Italianness and the long line of *contadini* I descend from, my ancestral history (as glimpsed in chapter 5) reveals another peculiarity. I am a Pentecostal. On both sides of the family, my grandparents belonged to and pastored churches for a Pentecostal denomination that I attended with my parents at a young age, before I can remember. Even though we belonged to a nondenominational church for the better part of my life, I have always been deeply Pentecostal. Growing up, we prayed like Pentecostals, upheld God's miraculous power like Pentecostals, and were conservative on most issues like Pentecostals. Nevertheless, my heritage's fuller significance was only illumined after intentional conversations with family and thumbing through inherited writings and family albums. Building a family tree and writing out this ancestral history has led to further discoveries about my religious roots.

The rich faith heritage of my family is emblematic of the "religious" Italian. Italians are frequently depicted this way. In the 1912 piece "In the Melting Pot: The Italians," an Italian American priest described Italians as "naturally and essentially a religious people."[6] A similar outlook was

---

4. Yong, *Future of Evangelical Theology*, 103.
5. See Hwang, "Confucianism in Modernization," 25–26.
6. Giambastiani, "In the Melting Pot," 9–10.

conveyed by a resident of late twentieth-century Italian Harlem: "We were taught two things: religion and we were taught family life. That was it."[7] The moral worth of Italians is tied fundamentally to their identity as Christians. Among the first generation of Italian Americans, this identity was explicitly linked to Catholicism. Someone who lacked or had lost their faith was considered "less than human."[8] Today, most Italian Americans identify as Roman Catholics, and the bulk of these regard themselves as devout adherents rather than casual observers.

Italy boasts a long history as a Roman Catholic nation. Indeed, Christianity in Italy reaches back to the first-century missionary ventures of the apostles Paul and Peter in Rome. The latter is revered as the first Bishop of the Catholic Church. Although the church faced severe persecution during its first three centuries, in 380 AD, under Emperor Theodosius I, the Edict of Thessalonica made Christianity the state religion of the Roman Empire.[9] Italy remains home to the Vatican, the hub of the worldwide Roman Catholic Church. While many migrant *contadini* seceded from the official church and joined other faith communities upon their journey to America, they retained, hardwired within, their fervent religiosity.

UNABASHEDLY PENTECOSTAL

As they built their lives in the New World, my ancestors embodied the faith-filled profile of Italians; however, they did so in an ecclesial context other than Catholicism. My paternal grandparents pastored churches in New York in Niagara Falls and, years later, on Syracuse's west side. Grandpa Palma served as the Niagara-Mohawk District Overseer (supervising about fifteen churches and forty ministers) and, for seventeen years, as the General Secretary of the CCNA. Grandma Palma was the District Director of the women ministries program and a gifted organist. My maternal grandparents pastored Bayside Church in Queens, New York. Grandpa Rubbo served as the Eastern District Overseer (with more than twenty churches under his charge) and as the secretary of *La voce della speranza* [The Voice of Hope] radio program. Grandma Rubbo was integral in organizing and developing the ministry departments at Bayside. On the occasion of her untimely passing in 1972, due to complications with illness, Grandpa remarked: "She will go down in history as the vessel God used most in our church to bring

---

7. Quoted in Orsi, *Madonna of 115th Street*, 77.
8. Cumbo, "'As the Twig,'" 53–54.
9. Wilken, *First Thousand Years*, 130.

the present to reality."[10] One begins to appreciate my Pentecostal heritage by looking at my grandparents' generation.

Reaching back one generation further, one gains a genuine sense of how deep my Pentecostal roots run. The common denominator among my great-grandparents—Michele and Catherina Palma and Massimiliano and Maria Tosetto (paternal), and Angelo and Carmela Rubbo and Vincenzo and Elisabetta Stigliano (maternal)—was the Italian American Pentecostal movement. As broached in chapter five, each emerged from their native background as Catholics to join the Pentecostal movement in America. Catherina and Massimiliano journeyed through transitional Waldensian and Baptist contexts, respectively. Still, each ended up as ministers of Pentecostal churches. And their church involvement was hardly one of passive attendance. Among my forebears, little precedent can be discerned of *nominal* (by name only) affiliation. Massimiliano and Michele were elected among the denomination's five original Overseers, and Catherina as the first Secretary-Treasurer. Massimiliano stood at the helm of the first national convention of the CCNA, held at his Niagara Falls (New York) church. Angelo and Carmela were integral in founding CCNA churches in New York City. Offspring of each the Palmas, Tosettos, Rubbos, and Stiglianos were active as ministers, and some as founders, of the CCNA.

My great-grandparents' active church involvement produced a subsequent generation (that of my grandparents) of leaders and ministers of the CCNA. While pursuing careers outside the church, my parents followed suit, remaining very much engaged in the life of the church. Both are actively involved in parachurch ministries today. I can't help that my family history reads like a "Who's Who" of the CCNA. The legacy of my ancestors is highlighted in the denomination's foremost history, the *Fiftieth Anniversary of the CCNA*.[11]

Once again then, my family profile appears to breach stereotypes. In addition to a tall frame and light complexion that belie my southern Italian origins, my religious background runs against the typical caricature of Italians as Roman Catholics. We remained devoutly religious (it's in our DNA), yet our denominational identity fomented within a Protestant context and one that only recently has achieved repute among mainline traditions. My Italian American Pentecostalness is thus entwined in a parody the casual observer might overlook. Yes, I am Italian; and though a third generationer, full-blooded. Yes, I am American; however, not of the

---

10. Rubbo, "Brief History," 2.

11. Galvano, *Fiftieth Anniversary*. See also Toppi, *E mi sarete testimoni*, 58–59, 69–70.

affluent, culturally-dominant northern European origins that my outward appearance might lead one to presume. Yes, I am a religious Italian, but neither I nor my parents nor grandparents affiliated with the Roman Catholic Church. Still, I have come to embrace my ethnocultural background. By looking at our roots, we can better understand why we think, feel, and act the way we do.

FROM THE OLD, INTO THE NEW

Among Italian émigrés of the Great Migration, the primary motive for leaving the country was economic. Harsh taxes, poor living and work conditions, and the late nineteenth-century agricultural crisis created incentive to explore new lands for opportunity and a future. Nevertheless, it would be reductionistic to say religion had nothing to do with the Italian peasants' journey to the New World. In Italy, the middle-class Catholic clergy have, for many years, allied with the landowning aristocratic elite. Among the *contadini* of southern Italy, the common perception of the clergy is that of a money-grubber, living off of peasant labors. *Contadini* tolerate this dysfunctional relationship, as the church is not the primary social institution around which the peasant builds solidarity. Loyalty to the family comes first. After family, solidarity at the village level plays an important role, and down the line after that is allegiance to the local parish. For the *contadini*, the church is seen chiefly as a place for christenings, marriages, and funerals. It is hardly the focal point of their communal spirituality. While peasants are religious, they look to patron saints and madonnas for an intermediary between them and God before seeking out the local priest. In the absence of an ecclesial emissary to plead their case, *contadini* follow a more mystical path of religious devotion, expressed primarily through rituals, chants, and charms. Their religion borders on magic, masking a protest of the official church's decrees, doctrines, and absolutions.[12]

The peasants of the Great Migration carried their age-old customs with them to the New World. Their core ideals stood in contrast with that of other Catholic peoples arriving in the United States simultaneously, such as the Poles (and other Slavs) who migrated with their village priests in tow.[13] *Contadini* saw no need for priests and even refused them when offered them by the Catholic hierarchy. One aspect of life they did import was their sacred *feste*—the feast days of patron saints. A *festa* is more than a religious service. It is a celebration, and, much to the clergy's chagrin, often held with

12. Vecoli, "Contadini in Chicago," 415–17.
13. Mangione and Morreale, *La storia*, 328.

processions and fanfare among large crowds on neighborhood streets. *Feste* remain integral to the social life of the *contadini* and in America, with Irish clergy looking on in disapproval, became a rather overt expression of the southern peasant's disdain for the official Catholic Church.[14]

In America, Catholic ethnic congregations eventually formed among the *contadini*, although with specific provisions made to accommodate the peasants' old-world ways. During the early years of their New World experience, many *contadini* turned to Protestant churches and a large number to Pentecostal and independent sectarian congregations. In fact, by the mid-thirties, Pentecostalism had emerged as the leading religious alternative among Italian immigrants. In 1936, the US Census Bureau accounted for only two Italian Protestant religious bodies, both Pentecostal—the General Council of the Italian Pentecostal Assemblies of God and the Unorganized Italian Christian Churches of North America (my family's denomination). Data collected from churches among the two bodies revealed a nationwide Italian Pentecostal membership of 11,114.[15] Presbyterianism, mistakenly regarded as the most significant Protestant work among Italian Americans, has been given considerably more attention. A study conducted on Italian Presbyterian churches (also drawing from 1936 data) accounted for a total membership of just 8,774 adherents nationwide.[16]

The Pentecostal church embodied freedom and emotionality, fulfilling a religious yearning denied the *contadini* by the hierarchism and dogmatism of American Catholicism.[17] The spontaneous, expressive style of Pentecostal worship bears a stronger resemblance to the peasant *feste* than it does to the official church's staid environment. For the peasantry, who comprised the bulk of Italian migration, Pentecostalism permitted a measure of continuity with their ancestral customs. For these reasons, my forebears gravitated towards the Pentecostal context in the New World. The timing of the Pentecostal revivals in Los Angeles and Chicago seamlessly corresponded with the wave of southern peasants of the Great Migration. When opposition from American Catholics threatened their old-world traditions, and it appeared there was no other religious alternative, the burgeoning Pentecostal movement filled the void.

Chicago's Assemblea Cristiana, the first Italian Pentecostal church on record, provided the tie that brought each set of my great-grandparents together in marriage. The people of the Assemblea Cristiana shared two

---

14. Orsi, *Madonna of 115th Street*, 55–59.
15. US Census Bureau, *Religious Bodies: 1936*, 747–48, 752.
16. Shriver, *Adventure in Missions*, 71–72.
17. R. M. Anderson, *Vision of the Disinherited*, 110–11.

things in common: dissatisfaction with the rigid structure of the Catholic Church and weariness of membership requirements levied by mainline churches. When congregants from the Assemblea Cristiana first visited the nearby North Avenue Mission, the epicenter of the Chicago Pentecostal revival, they welcomed the grassroots makeup and unscripted worship style they found. When subsequently pressed to structure the movement along denominational lines, the pioneers of Italian Pentecostalism adopted (in somewhat ironic fashion) the name the "Unorganized Italian Christian Churches of the United States." Thus, the initial effort to consolidate the movement's churches conveyed the persistence of a deep-seated anti-organizational sentiment. Any structure introduced at this stage was consented to reluctantly.

Contadini embraced the freedom they found in Pentecostal churches to read the Bible on their own accord. Well into the twentieth century, peasants (and the entire Catholic laity for that matter) were forbidden from reading Scripture. The Bible was considered a text of the clerics. Only those ordained to the church with the requisite training were permitted to read God's sacred Word. Penances, even excommunication, were enacted for those who embraced the Protestant call for all, clergy and laity alike, to read, study, and meditate on Scripture on their own accord. The Rubbos and Stiglianos (on my mom's side) were openly excommunicated from their church and disowned by their families and friends. Such treatment was extremely difficult for Italian immigrants who were already considered second-rate citizens.[18]

It was only with the Second Vatican Council (1962–65) and a new awareness for the responsibility of each member of the people of God, that the Catholic Church began condoning the reading of Scripture by the laity.[19] The loss of parishioners to Protestant contexts, where they could freely read the Bible, was one of the underlying motives for the shift in the Catholic Church's decrees. In his family history, *Hey God*, Italian American Frank Foglio describes the story of his family's journey from Catholicism to Pentecostalism. Foglio laments how his parish priest cautioned him from reading "that little black book."[20] Seen against the backdrop of Catholic restrictivism, reading and interpreting the Bible by the free-moving Spirit was very appealing to the migrant *contadini*.

---

18. Joy Palma, e-mail message to author, September 27, 2020.
19. Durasoff, *Bright Wind*, 191.
20. Foglio, *Hey God*, 16.

Italian Pentecostals harken to a longstanding Catholic mystical tradition, mediated through the folk-religiosity of the peasantry.[21] The famed patron saints of Italy, encompassing Francis of Assisi, Bonaventure, Catherine of Siena, and Thomas Aquinas, each embraced a direct encounter with God without the dogmatism that would typify Roman Catholicism in subsequent years. Among the exemplars of Italian Christianity in the thirteenth and fourteenth centuries, we find an unencumbered spirituality more akin to that of the Pentecostals. Catholicism had yet to codify in conciliar form various restrictions, such as the insistence that worship, absolution, and Scripture reading be mediated solely through the clergy.[22]

The life of St. Catherine reveals one enamored with "felt" religion. Catherine describes two defining moments in her spiritual journey: a "mystical espousal" (betrothal) and a "mystical death." The first experience consisted of a dynamic religious conversion, and the second, of a trance-like state where Catherine appeared lifeless to all observers for several hours.[23] The latter encounter resembles the rapturous experience exemplified in the Pentecostal "baptism in the Spirit." In his prolific outreach among the poor and the oppressed, St. Francis earned a reputation for his trenchant spirituality. Accounts exist of his ability to heal and speak in tongues, spiritual gifts commonly identified with modern-day Pentecostalism. Many of his followers in the Franciscan Order reportedly experienced the gift of tongues.[24] Italian spirituality through the ages draws from an opulent mystical tradition.

LETTING GO OF RESENTMENT

The Second Vatican Council inaugurated a new era, leading to several concessions on behalf of religious peoples once marginalized by the Catholic Church. Undeniably, the Council introduced a novel attitude toward

---

21. Alongside folk-Catholicism, Italian Pentecostalism also drew from Reformed revivalism (which shaped American Baptist and Presbyterian churches) and the Holiness currents that molded American Methodism. For more on the religious roots of the movement, see my *Italian American Pentecostalism*, chap. 1.

22. Such positions were adopted at the Council of Trent (1545–63) in response to the Protestant Reformation doctrine of the "priesthood of all believers." Livingstone, *Dictionary of the Christian Church*, 597; Chemnitz, *Examination of the Council*, 209–11.

23. Noffke, "Introduction," 4–5. See also Emling, *Setting the World on Fire*, 68.

24. Williams and Waldvogel, "History of Speaking in Tongues," 70–71; De Voragine, *Golden Legend* 149, 606; Hyatt, *2000 Years of Charismatic Christianity*, 60. On Italy's saints, including Bonaventure and Aquinas, see my book, *Italian American Pentecostalism*, 18–20.

Scripture. As stated by historian Tony Lane, "The Bible was let loose."[25] Other improvements included the reading of mass in the vernacular, no longer impugning Jews for the crucifixion of Jesus, and seeing both Protestants and Eastern Orthodox as "brethren" in need of prayer.[26] Moreover, a renewed emphasis on experiential religion was introduced, typifying the revivals leading to the Catholic Charismatic Renewal. The latter movement came onto the scene in the mid-sixties, initially among Catholic universities like Duquesne and Notre Dame. The Charismatic renewal became an extension, a new "wave," of Pentecostalism, now taking root within the older mainline churches.[27]

At the inaugural address of the Second Vatican Council on December 25, 1961, Pope John XXIII prayed for a "new Pentecost."[28] The advent of the Catholic Charismatic Renewal just a few years later was seen as the fulfillment of John's plea.[29] Efforts to reach across denominational lines became much more deliberate in the post-Vatican II era. Before the Council, Pentecostals in Italy were denied the freedom to worship. Pentecostalism was considered a movement that ran counter to the established religion of the state. At first, Pentecostals were tolerated, then subject to increasing persecution. Under the era of Mussolini Fascism, Pentecostals worshipping in public could expect to be arrested, imprisoned, and even executed.

From 1935 to 1955, the years the Buffarini Guidi circular was in effect, Pentecostals were forced to worship underground in cellars or in caves outside city lines.[30] The circular, drafted by Chief of Police Arturo Bocchini and countersigned by the Minister of the Interior, Guido Buffarini Guidi, ordered the immediate closure of all Pentecostal churches.[31] Public worship among Pentecostals was forbidden as "contrary to the social order and harmful to the physical and mental welfare of the race."[32] With the circular's lifting, Pentecostals gradually could move out into public spaces.

25. Lane, *History of Christian Thought*, 314.

26. Durasoff, *Bright Wind*, 191–92. Originally, the official label was "separated brethren," although ecumenism is wearing away at the "separated" connotations (191).

27. A. H. Anderson, *To the Ends of the Earth*, 211–12; Bartoş, "Three Waves," 33–34.

28. John XXIII, "Pope John Convokes the Council," 709.

29. Pope Paul VI, successor to John XXIII, explained John's plea as a "prophetic intuition" ("Gaudete in domino," under "VII. The joy of the pilgrim in this Holy Year"). See also Hughson, "Interpreting Vatican II," 16–17.

30. Bracco, "Italy's Most Crucial Hour," 2.

31. Toppi, *E mi sarete testimoni*, 62–64.

32. Translation of "contrarie all'ordine sociale e nocive all'integritá fisica e psichica della razza." *Buffurini-Guidi circolare*.

Vatican II set in stone the Catholic Church's new resolve to preserve the religious freedom of minority faiths in Italy and Catholic nations worldwide. On July 28, 2014, at the Evangelical Church of Reconciliation, Caserta, Campania, Pope Francis issued a public apology to Pentecostals for the decades of persecution, avowing:

> Among those who persecuted and denounced Pentecostals, almost as if they were crazy people trying to ruin the race, there were also Catholics. I am the pastor of Catholics, and I ask your forgiveness for those Catholic brothers and sisters who didn't know and were tempted by the devil.[33]

Admissions like this help me move past any resentment harbored for the abuses directed against the *contadini* and, subsequently, Pentecostals, at the Catholic Church's hands. I would be perpetuating the seeds of discord and enmity if I failed to acknowledge the Catholic Church's many strides since Vatican II. Harboring indignance only encourages the stereotyping that a recognition for our ethnocultural heritage ought to ameliorate.

In the narrative of Christianity, there is constant ebb and flow between oppressing parties, on the one hand, and those who rise within the ranks of the oppressed, on the other hand. For the Catholic Church, whether it was the promise of years off of purgatory via a monetary payment (the "indulgence" precipitating the Reformation) or the restriction of sacred Scripture characterizing the Tridentine era, there stands a remnant who choose to defend the subaltern and oppressed.

In *Growing Up African American in Catholic Schools*, Jacqueline Jordan Irvine and Michèle Foster examine the challenges some students face in specific contexts. Drawing from firsthand accounts, Irvine and Foster assess the history of marginalization and cultural incongruity of African Americans in Catholic educational institutions. In the fifties, Catholic schools in America were virtually all-white; however, in the wake of Vatican II, African Americans are finding a voice. Many report that they have found a supportive community and are making new strides because of the opportunities afforded by Catholic schools.[34] While some American ethnic groups have encountered adversity at the Catholic Church's hands (as a dominant religious and cultural entity), more revealing are the possibilities, moving forward, for cooperation and ecumenism with Catholic institutions.

While it is easy to do so, judging the whole of a religious institution or church by a part works against the tides of charity and restitution. Being

---

33. Zylstra, "Pope Francis Apologizes."
34. Irvine, "Lessons Learned," 170–71.

an active bridge-builder across the lines of denomination and tradition mirrors the onus to reconcile our present faith experience with our ancestral heritage. Rediscovering our family roots provides concrete opportunities for us to cross the dividing lines of denomination and affiliation. Even if we no longer identify with our forebears' religious views, we can choose to revisit this heritage as an opportunity for learning and growth.

Reflection Questions:

- Do your religious views today reflect the values of your ancestral heritage? What are some ways or beliefs your forebears exemplified that might enrich your present-day faith journey?
- Many of us harbor resentment towards others because of injustices we and our family, past or present, have experienced. In what ways can deepening our understanding of our faith heritage and that of those who have wronged us help us reconcile with others? Building bridges can begin with a simple prayer on behalf of those who have mistreated us.

9

What Makes Me Pentecostal

Miracles are not just purposeless and bizarre scientific oddities, but occur in such a way that purpose is attached to them by virtue of when and why they occur.

—Francis J. Beckwith, *David Hume's Argument Against Miracles*

I WAS SITTING BESIDE a woman at an English-speaking Pentecostal service. The congregation joined in song as the worship leader led from the stage up front. I heard the woman sing and gasp and utter words in what sounded like a foreign language. A moment later, a gentleman, several rows behind us, prayed aloud in English words of praise and reassurance. The woman who'd spoken in the strange tongue turned to the man and said, "You just put into English the heavenly words which I spoke from my heart. Now, not only me, but the hearts of the entire congregation are encouraged."

I value my Pentecostal roots. This heritage gave our forebears common ground and identity as new immigrants in America's ethnic enclaves. My ancestors encountered their share of marginalization in the New World, intensified by their native land's religiopolitical climate. At the hands of the new Kingdom of Italy, the pope had become a "prisoner of the Vatican."[1] Stirred with indignation, Pope Pius the IX banned Catholic participation in the public life of the Kingdom. From the pulpit, Catholic parishioners in America were taught the leaders of the Kingdom were bandits who had plundered the papacy. Zealous with allegiance to Pius and disdain for the Kingdom of Italy, many American Catholics ostracized Italian newcomers as jailers of the "Vicar of Christ." Moreover, they did so indiscriminately, without acknowledging that my ancestors (chiefly from southern Italy) wished no part in the affairs of the Kingdom.[2] The Pentecostal church offered confidence that, despite circumstances encountered in the New World, my ancestors had a network of support they could turn to in their hour of need. In the face of estrangement and excommunication, Pentecostalism represented a direct line to the approbatory love of their Creator. For these reasons, even long after joining a nondenominational church in subsequent years, we still treasure our Pentecostal heritage.

DO WE HAVE TO BELONG TO A PENTECOSTAL CHURCH TO BE PENTECOSTAL?

There were several underlying reasons for my family's shift from the Pentecostal context during my youth. The most apparent one is that the church we joined had more overlap with our respective social networks at work and school. Joining the new congregation, Eastern Hills Bible Church (New York), was also the way we expressed that our true loyalty was not to a single denomination but to our common faith (a significant step for our family). If someone asked me, or my siblings or parents, whether we consider ourselves Pentecostal, save perhaps some qualification, we would generally admit "yes." I know I would answer in the affirmative with little hesitation. Those like myself, who call themselves Pentecostals while belonging to other denominational (and nondenominational) churches, are often called *Charismatics*: or perhaps better, *renewalists* (a term I will explain in a moment). I prefer calling myself a Pentecostal. Doing so helps me identify with the tradition that brought so much to my migrant forebears as they built a way for themselves in America.

My siblings and I were not baptized in a Pentecostal church. Moreover, while my parents were baptized Pentecostal, they steered us to a nondenominational church growing up. Today, my folks and sister go to Baptist congregations, my younger brother attends a nondenominational

---

1. Vecoli, "Prelates and Peasants," 222.
2. Vecoli, "Prelates and Peasants," 222–28.

church, and my older brother is Presbyterian. My wife, kids, and I belong to the United Methodist Church (though we regularly visit our local Assemblies of God for the livelier worship). The trend among my family then, generally speaking, has been toward the older Protestant churches.

So why should someone call me a Pentecostal? Can a person be a Pentecostal without formally being a member of a Pentecostal church? It is increasingly acceptable today to refer to someone as a Pentecostal, regardless of where he or she attends church, as long as that person embraces a specific set of beliefs. These beliefs are rooted in the religious renewal catalyzed by the early twentieth-century Pentecostal revivals and fanned into flame among mainline churches through the Charismatic movement (beginning in the sixties). The terms *Pentecostal* and *Charismatic* (and the more generic, *Pentecostal-Charismatic*) can be used interchangeably to describe someone embracing this tradition. Perhaps the more fitting way to describe such a person is to call him or her a *renewalist*. The renewalist's distinguishing mark is the belief in the Holy Spirit's dynamic, ongoing work, chiefly through "spiritual gifts" (Gk., *charismata*).[3] These include the more ordinary "ministry" gifts such as teaching, preaching, encouragement, and evangelism, as well as the "miraculous" gifts, among which the most well-known are speaking in tongues, prophecy, and healing. "Speaking in tongues," in particular, is identified with Pentecostalism, an emphasis derived from the early Pentecostal revivals, which adopted speaking in tongues patterned on the early church model in the book of Acts. Early Pentecostals embraced the gift of tongues as the initial, outward "evidence" of a new empowering of the Holy Spirit, namely, the "baptism in the Spirit."[4]

DO WE HAVE TO SPEAK IN TONGUES TO BE PENTECOSTAL?

Some have gone so far as to say that someone is not a real Pentecostal until they have "spoken in tongues." However, this position has moderated with the worldwide expansion of Pentecostalism in recent years. A growing number of classical Pentecostals admit that they have never spoken in tongues.[5] Pentecostalism has developed immensely since coming onto the early twentieth-century scene as a fringe revivalist movement, isolated to a few US urban centers. Today, it is the second-largest family of churches

---

3. Rom 12:6, 1 Cor 12:31; Williams, *Renewal Theology*, 1:11–12.

4. Also referred to as the "Bible evidence." See Robeck, Jr., "William J. Seymour," 72–95; and Parham, *Voice Crying in the Wilderness*, 25–38.

5. Warrington, *Pentecostal Theology*, 87–88.

on the planet after Roman Catholicism with, according to one estimate, a global membership of more than 600 million.[6]

Sometime during my adolescent years, impressed by the vital portrait of the early church depicted in Scripture, I began pursuing a more profound experience of God's power. I sought a deeper, more direct encounter with the divine, beyond the routine weekly experiences programmed into my faith. In my prayer life today, I occasionally incorporate a *suprarational* experience, which some might label "speaking in tongues." Growing up, I can recall a handful of times when interspersed with our family's corporate prayers in English, someone prayed using an ecstatic form of speech. I describe such an experience as an *incomprehensible utterance*. For those who think speaking in tongues is merely mindless chatter and nonsensical babbling, an analogy is helpful. I liken such speech to the grunts, groans, and gasps of a fan cheering on their favorite sports team. Speaking in tongues does not imply abandonment of control at the altar of emotional expression, but it does mean availing oneself to the Holy Spirit communicating through them.[7]

According to the Bible, speaking in tongues is often accompanied by an "interpretation"—a rendering of the utterance in intelligible language. Paul is adamant that an interpretation should follow in a corporate setting. As expounded in First Corinthians, the purpose of such an interpretation is so that speaking in tongues—*glossolalia* (from the Gk. *glóssa*, "tongue," and *laleó*, "to speak")—always edifies the larger congregation (12:10; 14:5, 28). Uninterpreted *glossolalia* circumvents rational comprehension, hindering the gift's desired aim, namely, the edification of those present.[8] Even when tongues are spoken in private as a prayer language, Paul suggests one interprets them, lending intelligibility with one's mind (14:13–15).[9] While there is then an unintelligible, even ecstatic, dimension to speaking in tongues, an interpretation informing the intellect is meant to accompany the gift.

In the early days of the Pentecostal movement, accounts of speaking in tongues point to a more particular kind of speech known as *xenolalia*—words spoken in an unlearned foreign language and understood by one or more listeners standing by. According to Luke, the response among those gathered in Jerusalem to the first instance of speaking in tongues was utter bewilderment. As we find in Acts 2:

6. Johnson et al., "Christianity 2012," 29.

7. Williams, *Renewal Theology*, 2:396.

8. For an explanation as to why many Pentecostal congregations today practice speaking in tongues without the gift of interpretation, see Warrington, *Pentecostal Theology*, 88.

9. On the private nature of glossolalia in these verses, see also Fee, *First Epistle to the Corinthians*, 743–44.

> Each one heard them speaking in the native language of each. Amazed and astonished, they asked, "Are not all these who are speaking Galileans? And how is it that we hear, each of us, in our own native language? Parthians, Medes, Elamites, and residents of Mesopotamia, Judea and Cappadocia, Pontus and Asia, Phrygia and Pamphylia, Egypt and the parts of Libya belonging to Cyrene, and visitors from Rome, both Jews and proselytes, Cretans and Arabs—in our own languages we hear them speaking about God's deeds of power (vv. 6–11, NRSV).

Just as xenolalia accompanied Christianity's spread among the early church, it was present in Pentecostalism's expansion, enabling the gospel's communication across linguistic barriers. I am not sure whether I have ever experienced this form of the gift, either from the speaker's vantage point or as the hearer, but I believe xenolalia is possible today. Some would suggest that glossolalia always occurs in the form of a "real" personal language, whether human or heavenly (angelic), pointing to the belief that someone always understands our prayers.[10] Indeed, whether or not our prayers are intelligible to ourselves or someone else standing by, they are continually understood by God, who remains the object of worship.

In my college years, I became more intentional about the gift of tongues as a "prayer language" during personal meditation. For me, speaking in tongues has been chiefly a *devotional* experience, conducted in private before God (more than the *ministry* form of the gift, performed corporately).[11] I went to a Christian school, Wheaton College (Illinois), and as such, one could find other Pentecostals who claimed to speak in tongues, as well as Christians from a variety of backgrounds seeking the ability to do so for the first time. Part of college culture is experimenting with new things. At a Christian college, the desire to experiment often took on encounters of a "spiritual" nature. My friends and I read in Scripture, some for the first time, that ordinary people could experience the supernatural. Upon closer reading, it became apparent there was little reason to think that miraculous gifts were temporary (concluding after the apostolic age). The tenor of Scripture seems to run counter to such a *cessationist* hermeneutic. Seeing that Christian fellowship today should be modeled on the practices and teachings of the first-century church, many of us, instead, embraced a *continuationist* perspective, pursuing and praying for the miraculous gifts in our everyday lives.[12]

---

10. Cartledge, *Charismatic Glossolalia*, 69–70. See, for example, 1 Cor 13:1.
11. Williams, *Renewal Theology*, 2:397–98.
12. On the range of perspectives characterizing the cessationist debate, see Grudem,

One year, some of us were fasting after reading *A Hunger for God* by John Piper (a Wheaton alum and one of the most popular theologians among students). We learned that fasting might avail us of the profound spiritual satisfaction we were searching for.[13] The thinking behind the discipline was transparent—instead of consuming actual food at meals, we would focus during that time on the reality of God's Spirit as our source of inward, spiritual nourishment. After the fast, while praying with someone, it seemed that an incomprehensible utterance was shared. Moments later, I underwent an uncanny spiritual experience, an encounter much like the "mystical death" Catherine of Siena described. It was not something I could have fabricated or mustered up; it required little effort on my part. I very much took the seat of the recipient. For some time (perhaps hours), I laid motionless on my bed. Never had I felt so at peace or enjoyed such comfort. Whether this was the definitive "baptism in the Spirit" experience, I cannot say with absolute certainty. Glossolalia seemed to have been present, but it did not follow the usual pattern. The "tongues" phenomenon took place minutes before, perhaps even as the catalyst for the euphoric experience I have just described (not afterward as evidence of that experience). Still, of the spiritual encounters I have had in my life, either prior or since, this was the most profound.

Many spiritual experiences characterize the life of faith, attended with a vast range of feelings and effects. Perhaps sometime later in my faith pilgrimage, I will have another even more dynamic experience, which will become my defining "baptism in the Spirit" moment. Still, the exact name I assign the experience matters very little. Whether I call it "baptism in the Spirit" or, with St. Catherine, a "mystical death" is not of the essence. I am keen now to encourage others to pursue fuller intimacy with God, urging them to seek the "Spirit-filled" (i.e., Spirit-baptized) life in the same way I have done.

DO WE HAVE TO ESTEEM THE SUPERNATURAL OVER THE NATURAL TO BE PENTECOSTAL?

I have had encounters with miraculous gifts besides speaking in tongues, although these have characteristically been isolated and sporadic. On and off now for years, I have suffered from anxiety and depression, leading to many sleepless nights. My battle with insomnia has always come in waves. As a teen, amid a rather intense and prolonged bout, a prayer offered by

---

Systematic Theology, 1031–46.

13. Piper, *Hunger for God*, 61–62.

my mom seemed to lift the burden. In the following days and months, my disposition improved, and my sleep returned to a regular pattern. In another instance, I had suffered a knee injury in college playing recreational football. When I went for the MRI, the doctor said I had wholly severed a crucial ligament. I received a healthy dose of prayer when others saw me hobbling around on crutches and in the days immediately preceding surgery. During the operation, the doctor was surprised to find only a partial tear, one that would heal on its own. He removed some torn cartilage, stitched me up, and I was on my way to active form in a third of the time than initially forecasted. Such experiences keep alive my belief in the power of healing and continue to inform the way I pray for the sick and wounded today.

I have also witnessed the gift of prophecy. Though let me explain what I mean, as this particular gift is shrouded in misunderstanding. As depicted in the New Testament, prophecy is not always, nor normatively, tied to the *foretelling* of the future. I believe that prophecy patterned after what was typical among Old Testament prophets (foretelling) endures today, having read and heard accounts from reliable sources about future-oriented prophecies being fulfilled. Still, there is another kind of prophecy about which the New Testament speaks. On several occasions, someone has spoken dynamically into my life, as if encouraging me with the very words of God. This kind of *forthtelling* (rather than foretelling), pointed words given to admonish and encourage, resembles the type of prophecy Paul describes in 1 Corinthians 14:3: "Those who prophesy speak to other people for their upbuilding and encouragement and consolation" (NRSV).[14] We have all been encouraged by the words of others. However, this prophetic "speaking forth," although articulated via human words, seems to come directly from God and addresses specific concerns.[15] While not primarily future-oriented in scope, such encouragement offers consolation for anxiety and insecurities about what lies ahead.

I staunchly believe in the miraculous gifts and the possibility of direct, immediate encounters with the divine. Does this way of seeing the world make me less "modern"? Have I elevated the supernatural above the natural or, perhaps, retreated to pre-modern thinking? Ancient and medieval civilizations generally accepted, even took for granted, the reality of divine influence and supernatural causation.[16] I do not think I am guilty of relegating the natural to the supernatural and let me explain why. First of all, I am an academic. To undermine the reality of natural causation belies my critical

---

14. Williams, *Renewal Theology*, 2:384.
15. Storms, *Beginner's Guide to Spiritual Gifts*, 86.
16. Groothuis, *Truth Decay*, 33–35.

and investigative frame of mind. Several of my colleagues have written respected works on the integration of faith and science (i.e., the supernatural and natural).[17] While the miraculous emerges in space and time in real, although inexplicable ways, supernatural realities are neither ordinary nor normative. Miraculous phenomena are extraordinary precisely because they supervene ordinary, normal patterns. Moreover, natural explanations remain indispensable for describing the everyday processes of life.

The principle of *cause and effect*, woven into the fabric of the world around us, always yields observable and calculable results. As a theist, I believe God has ordered creation so that natural processes—perceivable cause and effect realities with expected explanations—are normative. Further, just as his presence and power are expressed through the supernatural, God's character and love are marvelously communicated through the natural. The familiar patterns of nature reveal the Creator's providential care, oversight, and sustaining influence. Maintaining a theistic worldview is not an affront to the law of causation, but instead implies ordinary causes are mediatory of God's constant and benevolent governance. Similarly, I accept the claim that the supernatural emerges in the midst of the natural from time to time. How else do we account for the many occurrences exceeding natural explanation in our lives, the lives of loved ones, or the many documented cases containing such events?

Perhaps you have heard lofty attempts to explain away allegedly miraculous phenomena. In many cases, the more rational approach, ironically perhaps, would be to admit to supernatural causation. Hematologist Jacalyn Duffin's encounter with the inexplicable fueled her study of supernatural healing and the canonization of saints. In the Roman Catholic tradition, for an alleged miracle to be deemed an actual miracle, a detailed investigation based on clerical, medical, and lay testimonies is conducted. Duffin's study of records stored at the Vatican Secret Archives identified more than 1,400 miracles since 1588. Based on her findings and belying her scientific background, Duffin concluded that miracles indeed exist.[18] Consider also the work *Miracles We Have Seen*, containing dozens of reports by America's leading physicians of unfathomable cures, resuscitations, and awakenings. Based on firsthand experience, medical experts describe unique events exceeding the grasp of modern science.[19] How do we reconcile such apparent anomalies, witnessed or confirmed by members of the medical community?

---

17. See Yong, *Spirit of Creation*; Ross, *Creator and the Cosmos*; and Vondey, "Does God Have a Place," 75–91.

18. Duffin, *Medical Miracles*, 3–7.

19. Rotbart, *Miracles We Have Seen*.

From a theistic standpoint, it seems God *allows* the supernatural to break into the natural, if only on occasion. When he does, he reminds those looking on that he is dynamically involved, still in the driver's seat, and ultimately responsible for the wonders we see around us in the created world. For these reasons, I must affirm the natural as normative and the supernatural as occasional yet meaningful.

CONCLUSION

From time to time, the inexplicable breaks forth in the midst of the ordinary: this may happen in prayer when ordinary words fail to convey our sorrow, pain, or longing, and so we erupt in incomprehensible cries and groans; in our conversations, when the words of another seem to convey the very voice and heart of an ever-present and personal God; or amid physical ailment, when inscrutable healings reveal God's compassion and power.

For me, being Pentecostal means valuing the Spirit's charismatic gifts and recognizing the legitimacy of the supernatural (although not to the exclusion of the natural). The Pentecostal church provided my ancestors a network of support amid profound changes brought on at the outset of life in the New World. In particular, it afforded a context in which my forebears could maintain a dynamic spirituality—one which Western society might seek to strip away. My Pentecostalness means it is okay to accept the occasional departure from ordinary, everyday happenings and remain enchanted by a God who often works "outside of the box." Rediscovering our religious roots offers a vital sense of identity and groundedness in an often superficial and trivial world.

Reflection Questions:

- Do you value the support of a local worship community? How does this community offer you and your family a sense of identity amid pressures to conform to the secular ideals of Western society? (If you don't have a place of worship, consider drawing up a list of spots, visiting some, and plugging in.)
- What role did the supernatural play in the life of your ancestors? What role does it play in your life today? Do you ever feel pressured by contemporary culture to downplay the miraculous?

PART III

Living Out Our Values

10

La famiglia

Listen, my son, to your father's instruction
and do not forsake your mother's teaching.
They are a garland to grace your head
and a chain to adorn your neck.

—Proverbs 1:8–9, NIV

SOMEONE MAY BE THINKING: "All of this about ethnic history and family applies to you because you're Italian. What about the rest of us?" Indeed, Italians have a reputation for their family centrism. And most would agree, this outlook is admirable. Consider the multitude of American television sitcoms initially conceived around the idyllic image of the Italian family: *Everybody Loves Raymond*, *Who's the Boss*, *That's Life*, and *The Fanelli Boys*, to name a few. Popular media admires cultures, like that of Italians, which appear to have transcended the modern erosion of the family.

One can attribute much of what is unfortunate about Western society to the erosion of family values. High divorce rates, and the rising number of single-parent homes and children born out of wedlock, mean that considerably fewer children than a generation ago grow up in a safe, stable, and nurturing environment. However, from this vacuity of values, society yearns for the forgotten ideal of the close-knit family. If the television interests of Americans are any indication, popular culture enshrines the emphasis on *la famiglia*. At the same time, there remains a notable divide between those enamored with an idyllic image of the family and the way American society functions.

WHEN FAMILY IS EVERYTHING

Within the Italian value system, the family is an "all-consuming ideal."[1] The family has always formed the core of my life. While I had plenty of friends growing up, the firmest ties in my life remained within the family. Despite their sometimes stern (yet mostly warranted) discipline, I always looked to Mom and Dad to guide me through the ups and downs of life. And I was quite close with my siblings, valuing and spending more time with my brothers and sister playing sports, video games, and building forts (while indubitably making a wreck of our basement) than I did with my friends.

One of our fondest memories was making home movies. We have hours and hours' worth of footage stowed away in my folks' video library. Not everyone had a video recorder in the eighties, so we rented one now and then. We recorded ordinary holiday traditions, various skits, and sometimes directed and starred in our own films. One of our favorite creations was a mafia crime drama. We even brought in my dad and grandpa to play the boss kingpins. Fortunately, "play" was never a scarce commodity for me as a kid.

As a family of six, statistically, we were about twice the size of the average American family.[2] My siblings and I are reasonably spaced out in age. There is a three-year difference between my older brother and me and seven years between me and my younger brother. I am closest in age to my sister (two years her senior). Being spread out in age gave us cause to create our own social networks outside the home. We never experienced rural life, out in the country, which would have necessarily distanced us from other families. We lived in DeWitt, in the heart of the suburbs of Syracuse, New York, with loads of other children around the neighborhood with which to play. Nevertheless, the bulk of my playful memories hinge around time with my siblings.

I grew up with a seemingly endless supply of sporting equipment, video games, remote control cars, water guns, Legos, and the like. There was never a dull Christmas or birthday in our household. The folks always

---

1. Giordano and McGoldrick, "Italian Families," 567.

2. The US family's average size in 1990 was 3.17 persons. US Census Bureau, *Abstract of the United States: 1991*, 45.

made sure we were outfitted with the latest craze of cutting-edge play stuff. The best way to manage four kids is to make sure they have loads of options to consume their time and energy. Among the possibilities were scores of books. With a teacher for a mom, it was a guarantee that there would be a plethora of books with which to fill our hours. As we matured, so did our reading interests, so the collections lining our bookshelves targeted our respective age groups. Reading time was networked into each day just before bedtime. On occasion, my dad shared a reading moment at dinner with a family reflection.

THE ITALIAN MOM AT CENTERSTAGE

I am grateful to my parents for how they instilled values into my life from an early age while cultivating a routine that promoted quality family time. My mom was the glue that held us together. While there is a patriarchal authority structure to most Italian households, the mother occupies center stage in the interior life of the home.[3] There were Mom's stellar cooking and the way she always ensured we had enough constructive activities to fill our days with. She brought unremitting energy and love, seeing the best in us while encouraging us to be even better. Mom nourished our faith with Bible stories and broadened our horizons with the very best books. She inspired us to explore and develop our interests in various areas, whether our scholastic pursuits, church involvements, or, among other interests, music. She encouraged each of us to take piano lessons (and we all did). In each area of life, Mom embodied the voice of encouragement. But most of all, she taught us to take pride in and enjoy our pursuits. If we lost our passion for a given venture, Mom never berated or pushed us against our will. She simply admonished us to put our energies elsewhere and explore other interests.

Mom has a knack like no one else I know for planning and throwing parties and get-togethers. I can't remember a dull birthday growing up. We had new cake creations and gifts each year, along with games and entertainment for friends invited over to celebrate. I will never forget my sixteenth birthday surprise party. Once again, Mom was the architect—behind my astonishment and the roaring fun. She recruited two of my close friends, a guy and a girl, who rallied what seemed like half the school (how they all ended up at our home without word getting out, I will never know). Mom never missed a beat when it came to graduation parties, and, for an educationally-minded family with four kids, there were many—I had four alone (including high school and each of my degrees). An ordinary celebration with just

---

3. Riccio, *Portrait of an Italian-American*, 85.

food and drink was never an option. There was always space set up outside for badminton, basketball, and bocce ball, with the basement cleared for billiards, table tennis, and our "hoops" arcade basketball game.

Mom usually rounded up people ahead of time to share a reflection or word of encouragement, alongside skits and the occasional good-spirited roast. For landmark birthdays, she perennially recruited my help. I became the go-to for a good roast, putting on my best impersonations (and not just for the guys). We have video clips of me satirizing my dad and grandpa, in addition to impersonating the ladies (dress and all!). The most epic impressions were of my Grandma Palma (Nona) at her seventy-fifth and Aunt Esther for her eightieth. We have shared many a laugh over the years rewatching clips, most recently with my wife and kids (it's a bit awkward explaining to your children how that's Daddy on the TV pretending to be your great aunt). Still, we enjoy the memories with laughter. And if everything else Mom did wasn't enough, there was usually a commemorative video she created with all the superlative clips of our youth. My folks' video library is teeming to the brim with memory tapes.

CAN WE LOVE OUR FAMILY TOO MUCH?

The family centeredness of Italians derives from the culture and living dynamics of the *Mezzogiorno*. The typical profile of the southern Italian family is that of a close-knit nuclear family and, in contrast to popular conception, significantly weaker ties among the extended family. Movies of Italian households filled with grandparents, aunts, uncles, and cousins living happily together under one roof are not accurate depictions of families in Italy's South. Large extended families living together is simply not viable in the typical one-room peasant home. Peasants characteristically live as tenants on the large estates (*latifondi*) of absentee landowners. Their subsistence lifestyle implies barely enough to sustain parents and children's basic needs, let alone the extended family.[4]

The vestiges of feudalism endure in southern Italy. In the South, for centuries, peasant villagers have worked the farms of wealthy landowners, taking only enough from their daily labor to sustain the needs of the immediate family. This labor is often carried out under a *sharecropping* obligation, assigning a given portion of the harvest to the owner.[5] Such families may have ties with extended (*parenti*) kin living elsewhere in the village, yet rigorous labor demands limit the ability to sustain bonds

---

4. Cinotto, *Italian American Table*, 51.
5. Cohen and Galassi, "Sharecropping and Productivity," 646–47.

outside the nuclear (*casa*) family.⁶ As a social institution, the *casa famiglia* remains intact in Italy and, arguably, more robust because of the nation's socioeconomic dynamics.

In *The Moral Basis of a Backward Society*, Edward C. Banfield paints a rather disapprobatory portrait of southern Italian culture. After living in a Sicilian village, Banfield concluded Italian peasants have a penchant for "amoral familism," a psycho-social condition consisting in the: "inability of the villagers to act together for their common good or, indeed, for any end transcending the immediate, material interest of the nuclear family."⁷ In other words, Banfield observed that peasants are so preoccupied with the concerns of the immediate family, they often neglect actions that might serve the interests of the village community as a whole. According to Banfield's theory, even when it was within their power to work toward the common village good, the peasantry's attention to the interior concerns of the family inhibited them.

Banfield's hypothesis is an intriguing one. It raises the question: Is it possible to care too much for our family's material needs? We have all watched movies or television shows where the storyline pivots on the conflict one character has between his or her responsibility to family, on the one hand, and the common good of society at large, on the other. Consider the television series 24, for example. In "Season One," counter-terrorist unit operative Jack Bauer, whose stated objective is to protect the welfare of the United States, at all costs, is presented by a terrorist with an ultimatum. In essence, Jack must give himself and his mission up in exchange for the life of his daughter. What would the ordinary person do in such a situation? If Jack forfeits himself and his mission, then the terrorist will likely succeed in his sinister plot (to kill a presidential candidate) and wreak incalculable havoc on the nation as a whole. If he resists, then his daughter dies.⁸ To put it another way, if Jack forfeits himself, he is acting in the interest of the greater good: ensuring the nation's well-being and saving potentially millions of lives. If Jack rescues his daughter, he safeguards that which is most dear to him, although he would have to carry on his conscience the sting of an untold loss of life.

Still, we are talking about a television show. Of course, Jack ends up dodging the consequences on either side, conceiving a plan that saves his daughter while at the same time ensuring the nation's security. What does a TV show tell us about Banfield's obscure notion of "amoral familism"? At the

---

6. Gabaccia, "Kinship, Culture, and Migration," 41–42.
7. Banfield, *Moral Basis*, 9–10.
8. Shapiro, "Episode 10:00 PM–11:00 PM."

least, the example from 24 teaches us to look outside the box and consider other available scenarios. Jack provides a model of healthy optimism—uncovering another option altogether, one that allowed him to account for the good of loved ones and society's common good in one stroke. Unfortunately, *contadini* (peasants) of Italy's South have never had the luxury of choice. Specific conditions have been reinforced in Italy over many years, stemming from the perennial subjugation and neglect of peasant interests, particularly, their pursuit of land reform. To his credit, Banfield clarifies the reasoning behind the peasants' "amoral familism," underscoring several conditions lying outside the peasants' control: a high mortality rate, landlord-imposed restrictions, and lack of means to sustain ties with extended family.[9] The centuries of marginalization are thus responsible for the apparent deficiency in the social constitution of the *contadini*.

Whether one interprets the southern Italian's family centeredness as a vice or a virtue, Italian culture remains esteemed in America for its family values. Americans idealize a pattern of behavior many *contadini*, in the face of marginality and exploitation, were forced to adopt out of necessity. Migration itself may be the crucial ingredient in buttressing the idyllic image of the strong extended Italian family.

IDEALIZING THE CLOSE-KNIT FAMILY

The limited means of the Italian peasant makes it difficult for entire families to migrate to the New World all at the same time. Most Italians arriving during the Great Migration were fathers and sons who hoped to earn a living in America and then return to their families in Italy with the bounty, possibly to purchase property of their own. The rate of return migration during this period, from America to Italy, was staggering. The Great Migration was the first largescale migration of people to the United States who went back to their native land in substantial numbers.[10] Indeed, after having tasted the fortunes of America, many migrants would, in subsequent years, journey back to the New World with their families in tow. For aid in passage to and at the outset of life in the New World, migrants turned to extended family and fellow villagers. High rent forced *contadini* into an unprecedented rate of cohabitation with extended family members. As a consequence of migrant life in America, the extended family filled the void of support that the nuclear family provided in Italy.[11]

9. Banfield, *Moral Basis*, 10.
10. Sowell, *Ethnic America*, 109–10.
11. Gabaccia, "Kinship, Culture, and Migration," 48–49.

The family-centric portrait of Italians blossomed on American soil through the transfer of Italian culture to the New World. The social structure of southern Italy supplied the foundation for the concept of the strong family unit. However, American popular culture has taken the close-knit Italian household image a step further—by enshrining it. This idealization may be understood, principally, as a reaction to Western culture's depersonalization and individualism.[12]

The relative success of the American way of life, particularly since WWII, has afforded a comfortability according to which the country's citizens may pursue their freedoms. Regrettably, this pursuit is carried out often to the neglect of the welfare of fellow citizens. Professor of History and Political Science at Syracuse University, Ralph Ketcham, argues the nation's political system caters to absorption with private interests. A system that defers in the public sector to elected representatives, as "guardians of special interests," tends to shift attention from civic virtue to the individual's isolated interests. Explains Ketcham: "Once politics is defined negatively, that is, seen as a means merely for protecting or enhancing private interests, then explicit public concerns become secondary or even non-existent."[13] The rise of terrorism since Ketcham made this argument has curbed the apparent rise of comfortability, but America's political structure has changed very little. As public concerns become dominated by individual gain, society craves more than ever an interior life structured around the healthy family.

One can point then to given historical dynamics and the blending of cultures to explain the idyllic image of the Italian family. The broader cultural sentiment enshrining this image means that America is one step nearer to realizing the ideal of the close-knit family and recovering the nation's core values.

VITAL INGREDIENTS: FOOD, FELLOWSHIP, AND FUN

I remain grateful for all that our family had growing up. Nevertheless, much more than the material blessings, in our household certain built-in activities and structured events reinforced family values. Moreover, while our Italian background informed such endeavors, these remain activities nearly any family can adopt. A household can gauge their strength by how well they incorporate the *thriving family's three F's*: food, fellowship, and fun.

Integral to the thriving family is having a set time for dinner. Recent studies suggest the average number of family meals among US households

12. Cinotto, *Italian American Table*, 58.
13. Ketcham, *Individualism and Public Life*, viii.

is in decline, with such meals constituting less than four a week. This downward trend has had a detrimental effect (particularly among children) on diet quality, weight, and psychosocial function.[14] Italian food culture pivots on a scheduled dinner time. Growing up, we protected our Sunday dinner—the high point of each week, both from a culinary standpoint (with the best fixings reserved for Sundays) and from a communal or social one. Likewise, each day the rest of the week, we had our set five o'clock dinner, with little exception. When I was a little older, we looked forward to a Friday night meal out on the town at one of our favorite spots.

We had embraced the essence of the Italian "food ritual," carrying significance on several levels. Our regular mealtimes provided a sense of constancy amid the hustle and bustle of American life. Moreover, as an immigrant family, our dinner routine facilitated intimacy and underscored the strides our family had made in the New World. The dinner tradition embodied a celebration of our migrant forebears' success, who had emerged from scarcity to wealth and stability. Writing on Italian American families of East Harlem, historian Simone Cinotto describes the underlying meaning of the Italian dinner tradition:

> Abundance and conviviality were in the meal the most tangible expressions of the dream of immigrants who had known only scarcity. The relatively frequent consumption of meat, pasta, white bread, coffee, and sugar, foods that immigrants had only dreamed of in Italy, had revolutionary implications, signaling the breakdown of a long-standing class barrier. Liberated from the chains of scarcity, cooking was the only feature of immigrant material culture that could fully blossom in the new urban world. Food rituals told success stories.[15]

As we gathered around the table, the feast that lay before us symbolized victory. The bountiful meal conveyed triumph, expressing the success of a people who originated in Italy with very little and, after the toils of passage, arrived in the New World with even less. Through adversity, my ancestors charted the economic ladder in America, from the very bottom on up.

The Italian dinner tradition taps into a custom valued across religious traditions. The practice of "table fellowship" remains a cornerstone among many faith contexts. When understood against the backdrop of the Lord's Supper tradition, corporate mealtimes carry sacramental worth. As the preeminent church sacrament, the Eucharist was built on the values of

---

14. Neumark-Sztainer et al., "Changes in the Frequency," 204; Berge et al., "Similarities and Differences," 99–101.

15. Cinotto, *Italian American Table*, 51.

fellowship and sharing embodied in corporate mealtimes.[16] The need to clearly define expectations at corporate meals spurred the first-ever Christian council. The apostles convened the Jerusalem Council (depicted in Acts 15) to address obstacles impeding table fellowship among Jewish and Greek Christians. Greek Christians were entreated to abstain from blood products, as such foods went against the Jewish people's dietary laws. In return, Jews were discouraged from demanding Gentile believers be circumcised. Indeed, the favorable European attitude towards blood products (e.g., blood sausages) led to a severe rift among the early Italian Pentecostals. While some cleaved to their blood sausages, others, interpreting the Jerusalem Council's admonitions literally, pointed a finger in disrepute upon the *manga-sangue* (blood-eaters).[17]

The practice of table fellowship can be found in other religious contexts. While some think Judaism's kosher food laws reinforce legalism, there is a deeper level of meaning to them. Jewish food customs form the foundation of the celebratory Hebraic *Shabbath* (Sabbath) meals. On the *Shabbath* (beginning sundown Friday and ending sundown Saturday), Jews look forward to not one but two fellowship meals. As Arlene Rossen Cardozo explains, on Friday evening after *shul* (synagogue), Jews enjoy the "finest meal of the week." As the tradition developed, once again, on Saturday afternoon, Jews enjoyed "a Sabbath lunch followed by a long nap."[18] In Islam, during the month of Ramadan, families fast during the day and gather immediately after sunset for an evening meal (Ar., *iftar*) to break their fast together. *Iftar* commemorates the example of Islam's founder, Muhammad, and is often celebrated with dishes reserved only for Ramadan.[19]

There is no better way to foment family ties than weekly involvement with our local congregation. Growing up, come Sunday morning, everyone in the household was in sync: after waking up, having breakfast, and dressing up in our Sunday's finest, we loaded into the car for a fifteen-minute trip to the other side of town for weekly worship. While going our separate ways for Sunday school, we enjoyed the main service together. Many other involvements at church, scattered throughout the week and over the year, brought us together: musicals, Vacation Bible School, and my dad's church-league softball games. Our household today emulates

16. Hess, "Befriending Outsiders," 81–88.

17. For a detailed discussion of the impact of the "Blood Issue" on Italian Pentecostalism, internationally, see my article, "Between Abstention and Moderation," 14–24.

18. Cardozo, *Jewish Family Celebrations*, 8.

19. El-Zibdeh, "Understanding Muslim Fasting Practices," under "Fasting in Ramadan."

this Sunday routine and other such involvements: this year, the kids participated in children's choir, VBS, and in years past, I even donned the old glove and cap for the church softball team.

Among other activities cementing quality family time as a kid were various leisure outings and vacations. We looked forward to a family getaway a few times a year and always during summer. Some of my oldest and fondest memories were of our annual outdoors retreat with another family in the mountains of upstate New York. We enjoyed fishing, hiking, and swimming during the day while huddling up around the fire for board games at night. When we were a bit older, my dad and uncle bought a cottage in the Adirondacks, where we enjoyed many of the same activities during weekend getaways spread out over the year. It was a quiet lake, so no motorboats, but excellent bass and pickerel fishing and plenty of time to soak in the fresh air, reflect, and enjoy the beauty of the outdoors.

Now a husband and father, I aspire to the same family-centric customs, insisting on routine mealtimes together, regular involvement at our local place of worship, and recurrent leisurely getaways. Although my wife and I are distanced from close family (our parents, on both sides, residing at least nine hours from us), we structure our family trips around the prospect of seeing our parents, siblings, and extended family.

Reflection Questions:

- As you look back on your ancestral history, would you say that contemporary culture has fortified or eroded your and your kin's core values?

- Everyone struggles with how to prioritize family time amid their daily and weekly routines. How can you be more intentional about integrating the *thriving family's three F's* (food, fellowship, and fun)? What steps can you take to incorporate regular mealtimes together, weekly worship, and family leisure activities?

11

Navigating Gender in Home and Church

There is neither Jew nor Gentile, neither slave nor free, nor is there male and female, for you are all one in Christ Jesus.
—Galatians 3:28, NIV

AT THE DINNER TABLE growing up, generally, the women cooked, and the men prayed. Suppose one were to take this dinner tradition as a paradigm for the way we lived the rest of our lives. In that case, one might presume that our home was patriarchal, as with most Italian households. If one extends this line of thinking, other questions emerge: Did we consciously think of our home as a patriarchy? If so, might my parents have structured the family any differently? How did our religious identity as Pentecostals inform the structure of our home?

I admit that, in some respects, our family tilted in a patriarchal direction. While in subsequent years, my mom fulfilled her career aspirations, early on, she stayed at home with the kids. Again, one might presume we perpetuated the patriarchal stereotype because Mom stayed home while Dad worked. On the other hand, one could argue that my mom did the share of the cooking because she was the better cook. Or, consider the underlying motivation for the dinner prayer tradition: Did the men pray as a demonstration of spiritual headship, or is it basic etiquette that the blessing for a meal comes from someone other than the person who prepared it?

The question of patriarchy remains a perplexing and controversial one. The United States is still a patriarchal nation by and large; however, there is evidence of a shift in recent years. It was not until the seventies that married women in the United States could legally use their maiden name. While the vast majority of US-born married women use their husband's last name, the percentage using a surname different from their husband's (e.g., a maiden or hyphenated name) is increasing.[1] Historically, males have occupied a more significant share of the US labor force, although, once again, we see a shift in recent years. In 1950, approximately one in three women participated in the labor force. According to the US Bureau of Labor Statistics, as of 2015, over half (about 57 percent) of women work.[2] Another study reveals that in more than half of American families today with children, women are the dominant parent. This statistic encompasses, and is perhaps tilted by, the many single-parent households where a father figure is all-together absent.[3] Nevertheless, these trends point to a surge in the number of children growing up in matriarchal homes.

Truth be told, my dad is an excellent cook. He's the outdoor grill specialist (a duty I aspire to today). As part of family tradition, Dad always prepares the Thanksgiving turkey and the Christmas roast (a tradition we maintain in our home). He even dabbled in pizza-making for a time (with a specialty anchovy pie). And for his part, my dad helped shoulder the responsibilities of looking after four kids. Before I could drive, Dad was usually the one who picked me up from sports practice. Multiply that by four kids, and we were typically two-season athletes, and the number of post-practice pick-up trips adds up over the years. In the same vein, Mom sometimes says the dinner prayer. Moreover, for a good part of my life, she was a breadwinner alongside Dad.

So then, our family occasionally turned the stereotypical profile of the Italian household on its head. Doing so was our way of saying that specific cultural norms needn't define how we do things. Mom and Dad had their manner of managing work, dinner, and child responsibilities. Both accepted their obligations willingly and, I venture to say, would do it the same way all over again.

1. P. Cohen, "America Is Still a Patriarchy," under "Patriarchy."

2. Bureau of Labor Statistics, "Women's Share of Labor Force"; Bureau of Labor Statistics, "Women in the Labor Force."

3. Russell, *Master Trend*, 121–22.

"BE SUBJECT TO ONE ANOTHER"

Our Italianness unmistakably informed the family dynamics of our home. Were we more patriarchal than most American families because of our Italian roots? It would be fair to say that our Italian cultural heritage *predisposed* us to a patriarchal structure more so than the average American family. Italy is more patriarchal than America and most countries. While women in Italy are beginning to hold educational training and job qualifications comparable to men, the country's percentage of females participating in the workforce remains lower than that of the United States and Britain.[4] A study by the ethnologist Salvatore Cucchiari reveals that some southern Italian households function according to a "domestic matriarchy," whereby the mother's authority inside the home rivals that of the father. Nevertheless, the influence of women remains mostly confined to the domestic sphere. In public, women in Italy are expected to defer to the headship of their husband.[5]

My parents exhibited many qualities consistent with *egalitarianism* (supporting equality in the home). In addition to the exceptions to patriarchy previously noted, Mom and Dad always looked to one another before reaching a conclusion when it came to important decisions. When broaching a concern that involved one of the kids, they typically approached us as a unified team. Today, my wife and I strive to model our own home on the same values, consulting with one another first on decisions where family welfare is at stake. While weighty decisions may not occur every day, I can think of few things more integral to family life than maintaining time each day to talk or pray with our spouse. Doing so builds a routine so that when significant concerns come up, we are ready to talk it through.

How could a family like the one I grew up in embody egalitarian values—especially when doing so would seem to belie not only our Italianness but specific stereotypes of Pentecostal culture as well. Combining our Italian roots with the biblically conservative, literalist leanings of Pentecostals would seem like a recipe for patriarchy. Historically, Pentecostal churches have favored men for ecclesial leadership positions, allotting limited authority to women, such as overseeing women or children's groups. If one adopts a firm literalist stance, it is not hard to conclude, for instance, that the Bible instructs women not to teach over a man. A literal interpretation of specific passages suggests that women should remain silent in church and not voice their concerns in a public setting. According to the admonishment of Paul:

---

4. Miller, "Demography and Gender Regimes," 201.
5. Cucchiari, "Between Shame and Sanctification," 687.

> Women should be silent in the churches. For they are not permitted to speak, but should be subordinate, as the law also says. If there is anything they desire to know, let them ask their husbands at home. For it is shameful for a woman to speak in church (1 Cor 14:34–35, NRSV).

However, the biblical emphasis remains that of equality. The very first chapter of Scripture upholds the shared identity of men and women in the *imago Dei*: "So God created humankind in his image, in the image of God he created them; male and female he created them" (Gen 1:27, NRSV). Among all creation, humanity alone—male and female alike—bears the divine nature's imprint. Men, alongside women, uniquely possess the ability to feel, think, and reason.[6] As the new covenant community, the church is rooted in shared identity in Christ (Gal 3:28). Controversial passages, like Ephesians 5:22 ("wives, be subject to your husbands," NRSV), must be interpreted within the broader context of biblical equality. Indeed, Paul frames his pericope on the foundations of the godly household in chapter 5 by the principle of mutual submission: "Be subject to one another out of reverence for Christ" (v. 21, NRSV). Husbands are asked to be subject to wives, as are wives to husbands, out of an attitude of Christ-like devotion.

SERVING AGAINST THE GRAIN

Traditionally, Pentecostal churches have favored males in positions of church leadership. Nevertheless, such a patriarchal structure does not imply authoritarianism or that Pentecostal women perceive men as acting in a domineering way towards them. Some Pentecostal women actively encourage men to accept the responsibility of moral leadership in the family and church. Florence Crawford (1870–1936), for example, founder and leader of the Pentecostal denomination, the Apostolic Faith Mission (Portland, Oregon), demanded husbands and fathers assume the role of headship within the home. She maintained that glad and willful submission on the part of the wife was necessary, redeeming a God-intended paradigm and serving the family's best interest. Taking her cue from the biblical portrait of womanly responsibility in the church, Crawford challenged existing social hierarchies by insisting that women preach. She was a formidable evangelist in her own right.[7] In this way, Crawford also became a forerunner of the trend to egalitarianism among Pentecostal churches.

---

6. Chandler, *Christian Spiritual Formation*, 31–32.
7. Deno, "God, Authority, and the Home," 83–105.

In Pentecostal churches, women increasingly occupy pastoral positions (including posts with men under their charge) and are certified and ordained as ministers. In most Pentecostal congregations, women are encouraged to take the pulpit if endowed with speaking gifts. For example, in historically Italian Pentecostal denominations, including the Christian Church of North America (CCNA) and the Canadian Assemblies of God (CAG), women enjoy ordination opportunity. Some even serve as head pastor.[8] A similar trend is evident among Latina/o Pentecostal churches in the United States. By the eighties, for instance, Latina ministers in the Assemblies of God were not only being ordained; they were inhabiting lead pastoral and administrative positions.[9] Pentecostal ecclesial contexts thus facilitate egalitarian sentiment among historically marginalized ethnicities in the United States.[10]

Among my parents, my mom is the better speaker (and my dad would agree). Since she retired from teaching, she has pursued a ministry calling that allows her to use her speaking gift in an itinerant capacity. She often travels to conferences and churches around the country to teach, admonish, and inspire—women and men alike. Although reaching a nondenominational audience, her work includes venues among Baptist churches (to which my folks currently belong). Baptists have long favored males in speaking and ministerial positions.[11] Consider also my great-aunt Esther, who served for many years as an itinerant minister for the CCNA. Her focus and passion was youth work, yet her travels brought opportunities to speak before entire congregations, with her admonishments falling on the ears of men and women alike. My mom and aunt are examples of the trendsetting minister, moving against the grain in Christian contexts that have traditionally veered in a patriarchal direction.

CONCLUSION

Although exhibiting attributes of a patriarchal structure (and despite our Italian Pentecostal background), my family also demonstrated egalitarian values in day-to-day life. In an age when the LGBTQ movement and the introduction of new terms (*transgender, transsexual, intersex, cisgender,*

---

8. See my book, *Italian American Pentecostalism*, 181–82.
9. Espinosa, "Your Daughters Shall Prophesy," 38–39.
10. See Cumbo, "'Your Old Men,'" 47–48.
11. This is particularly prominent among churches affiliated with the Southern Baptist Convention, comprising the considerable majority of US Baptists. See Southern Baptist Convention, "Baptist Faith and Message," art. 6.

gender dysphoria, among numerous others) challenge the traditional meaning of gender, it may be time to pursue more innovative ways of discourse about household roles. A recent proposal offers a middle ground between *hierarchism* (i.e., patriarchal or matriarchal models) and egalitarianism. Biola University professor Michelle Lee-Barnewall suggests a "servant leadership" approach that emphasizes "servanthood," rather than merely using the word "servant" to temper the more predominant idea of "leadership." She maintains that being a "servant" is critical to the essence of leadership, as one seeking to emulate Christ's self-giving love.[12]

The subject of gender in family and church demands a more nuanced and compassionate understanding of identity.[13] Perhaps the language of "roles" itself is becoming outmoded. In our household, it was never as much about roles, per se, but about using our God-given abilities to better the family. A focus on our respective giftings, rather than roles, might help emphasize the portrait of Christian unity that Paul had in mind in Ephesians. Our respective roles, offices, and responsibilities derive from the gifts bestowed in the one Spirit: "for works of service, so that the body of Christ may be built up" (4:12, NRSV).

Reflection Questions:

- Growing up, what responsibilities did your parents carry out within your household? Did these functions support or subvert traditional stereotypes (e.g., the man as the breadwinner and woman as the cook)? Would you consider the home you grew up in to be more patriarchal, matriarchal, or egalitarian in structure? In hindsight, related to your growing up years, what have you learned about gender roles?

- How do your household responsibilities today support or subvert traditional stereotypes (for those not yet married but planning to, what respective functions do you envision for you and your would-be spouse)?

---

12. Lee-Barnewall, *Neither Complementarian nor Egalitarian*, 103–4; the patriarchal model is generally assumed by those advocating biblical *complementarianism*. Blomberg, "Neither Hierarchicalist nor Egalitarian," 326.

13. Murray, *Saving Truth*, 145–51; and Mehra, *Brown White Black*.

12

Towards a Holistic Approach to Well-Being

Do not conform to the pattern of this world, but be transformed by the renewing of your mind. Then you will be able to test and approve what God's will is—his good, pleasing and perfect will.

—Romans 12:2, NIV

I came to realize the importance of rediscovering who we were *made to be* after a personal bout, over many years, with mental illness. In my early twenties, I was formally diagnosed with an anxiety disorder, for which presently I receive medical treatment. For me, the chief symptom of the condition is insomnia. As far back as I can remember, I have had problems sleeping. As a child, we wondered if I was particularly sensitive to caffeine in beverages and chocolate products, so I limited my intake. Yet, the sleeplessness ensued. As an adolescent, my insomnia became more intrusive. The sleeplessness seemed to come in waves, with sometimes many months passing without any problem, followed by another bout of several weeks or even months. In subsequent years, I found that learning about my ancestral-identity was an essential part of achieving the peace of mind God wants for all his children.

CAUGHT IN A VICIOUS CYCLE

I have always had a very active mind, exceedingly conscious of my thoughts. I am prone to the vicious cycle of worry. I can remember "thinking about thinking" (as strange as that might sound), perplexed by the reality that the more I tried to stop thinking about something, the more that particular something became a preoccupation and, inevitably, the more I thought about it.

During middle school, my worries turned to what others thought of me, and although this is normal for an adolescent, the disruptive behavior patterns that followed were not. It was not uncommon for me to stir with worry the entire night, with all but an hour or two of sleep, and then get up and go to school the next day. The lack of sleep affected the way I felt about myself and my impression of how others viewed me, in turn, perpetuating the vicious cycle of worry. Typically, after a few weeks to a month, the bout of anxiety and insomnia would subside. The pressure and loss of sleep corresponded to stress at school. I placed exceptionally high expectations on myself: academically, athletically, and interpersonally. I wanted as much as possible to please my parents, teachers, coaches, and peers.

Still, the waves of sleeplessness continued into high school, dictated by anxiousness over performing well for those around me, myself, and even God. By the time college rolled around, I had tried just about everything: chamomile tea, anti-acids to calm the stomach, melatonin sleep aides, and other over-the-counter remedies. But to no avail. Frustration set in—I spent hours on end with my thoughts, night after night, staring at the ceiling, trying by the sheer power of will to fall asleep.

During college, I had my first panic attack. The sudden onset of intense apprehension led to a loss of consciousness. As I felt my heart rate escalate, I put my head between my legs and, the next thing I knew, was waking up on my dorm-room floor in a daze. The pattern of anxiety and sleep loss became severe enough that I decided it was time to join the roughly 17 percent of Americans who take some kind of a psychiatric drug for their problems.[1] The psychiatrist started me on a low dose of a Selective Serotonin Reuptake Inhibitor (SSRI). I tried this for about a year before realizing it didn't sit well. I began to skip doses—something anyone well-informed about SSRIs will caution you concerning. The resultant erratic behavior eventually landed me in an inpatient mental health clinic for a week, where staff monitored and regulated my treatment. It was during this weeklong stay that I was diagnosed with an anxiety disorder.

---

1. Fox, "One in 6 Americans."

I came out of the clinic on a cocktail of pills: a new SSRI, a low-dose sleep aide, and a benzodiazepine (for short-acting treatment of occasionally intense anxiety). In the aftermath of the hospital stay, I spent a year at home in Syracuse. While it was good to be in familiar surroundings with a robust support system, I struggled to adjust to life on the high dose of medication the clinic had prescribed. The combination of lingering sleeplessness and aggravating side-effects prompted experimentation with a half-dozen other prescriptions, numerous pill cocktails, and dosing fluctuations to ad nauseam.

Although I did my best to move forward with work, graduate studies, and life as usual, after several years, it became apparent that I was still taking too much medication. I often felt lethargic, lacking interest in activities I once enjoyed. Subsequently, albeit under the oversight of my psychiatrist, I cycled off one of the medications completely. I say "oversight," even though this amounted to one 15-minute visit every six months. Each time I was with the doc, I asked if I could taper down on the drug, to which he recurrently replied, "you are free to try if you like." Unfortunately, this was the extent of the instruction. There was no warning one would expect to hear, like, "if you start to feel such and such a way, call or come see me as soon as you can." This trial period met with disastrous results. I eventually weaned off the pill entirely. Sleep loss and anxiety set in and proceeded to escalate. I found myself getting worked up over everyday decisions, with intense moments of stress over: What clothes to wear? What foods to eat? And whether to go to the gym and work-out?

I was forced to take medical leave from my job, during which time I returned to my previous drug regiment and, perhaps more importantly, changed psychiatrists. My new doctor encouraged me to come in and meet as often as every month. I suspected I was still on too much medication. The more regular and not so rushed appointments with my new psychiatrist provided a more stable environment. I tapered down on the drugs and, this time, did so much more gradually. The doctor took the time to counsel me on each medication's purpose. It has been several years since then, and my mental and physical health has steadily improved.

MORE THAN CHEMICALS

I have finally found the stability, medically-speaking, I had hoped for when I began treatment for mental illness more than fifteen years ago. I have had my share of ups and downs, and even some monumental peaks, along the way. I met and married my one true love. We had three beautiful children.

I earned a master's and a PhD and have had my work published in multiple venues. I am now experiencing some lasting stability. Looking back, part of me wonders whether I should have gone on any psychiatric medication in the first place. Of course, this a moot point now. I have come to terms with the fact that I have a biochemical imbalance—my body simply does not process as it should *serotonin* (a neurotransmitter tied to various cognitive functions and a sense of well-being and happiness).[2] I am now stable on just one psychiatric prescription: an SSRI (and a lower dose of it). Nevertheless, it remains clear that the medical explanation for my struggle, by itself, is inadequate.

Our experiences either reinforce or, more often, cause us to repress, trivialize, and reject aspects of our ancestral-identity. Racial discrimination and other forms of prejudice, for example, add incentive to suppress or ignore facets of our family heritage.[3] Intentionally tracing our roots enables a needed sense of continuity with our ancestral background, illumining why we think, feel, and behave in specific ways. Activities such as conversations with loved ones, perusing family records (written and photographic), and building a family tree help us reconstruct our identity. An increasingly used and productive practice among psychologists is having patients build a *genogram* (a graphical representation of their family relationships). As with a family tree, genograms help patients map their family history, engendering insight into genetic and behavioral patterns.[4]

Tying the process of rediscovery to the social fabric of family is essential. Introspection can add fuel to the fires that cause us to ignore or repress our roots. As someone prone to this kind of thinking, I can tell you that there are two sides to the introspective personality. On the one hand, when introspection fosters a meditative outlook and heart-searching, it can be very productive. On the other hand, introspection can lead to self-absorption and unhealthy rumination. Everyone experiences the vicious cycle of worry (although perhaps some more than others) by which one's mind fixates on their performance and the way others view them. Performance anxiety can lead to nervousness, lack of confidence, and the disruption of necessary behavior patterns like sleep and eating. The effect can be under-performance, declining interest in one's social life, or the inability to relate and work productively alongside others. As the vicious cycle ensues, it causes one to, in turn, think and worry about life even more.[5]

---

2. Martin and Hine, *Dictionary of Biology*, s.v. "serotonin."
3. Perez and Hirschman, "Changing Racial and Ethnic Composition," 10.
4. Christine Clark, "Genogram," 584–85.
5. On the vicious cycle of worry (and the related condition of depression), see Widdowson, "Avoidance, Vicious Cycles," 198–99.

Our mental health is inextricably tied to the quality and wellness of our relationships. Humans, like all creatures, were made to function best in a social environment. As social beings, life entails both giving and receiving—cultivating our abilities with the good of others in view, on the one hand, and being willing to accept from others aid to live meaningfully and productively, on the other hand. As the most basic social unit, rehabilitating and fostering healthy family relationships is critical. Such a precedent follows the relational (social) model of the Trinity. The Triune God is a family of inter-reliant persons—Father, Son, and Spirit—joined in tandem in an eternal, symbiotic dance of giving and receiving. God's intention, from the beginning, was that our earthly family should reflect this intra-trinitarian love. As Professor of Christian Formation and Leadership at Regent University, Diane Chandler, suggests, by God's design: "The family was to be an incubator of godly love and the primary conduit for Christian formation." Our family, intended to embody God's Triune love, is the starting ground for our relational health.[6]

Some are more prone to emotional instability than anxiety, which impacts our relationships and how we function day-to-day. Overprescribing anti-depressant, mood-stabilizing, anti-psychotic, and other psychiatric medications to treat anxiety and life's ups and downs is an increasing problem. Resorting to drugs, to the neglect of techniques like the faith-affirming and family-building approach I have advocated in this book, can "medicalize" the patient. Overprescribing has several consequences: it may turn a short-term problem into a chronic disease; foster an overreliance on medical experts, impeding the sufferer's ability to "self-regulate" (take proactive steps to improve); or place the patient at risk for debilitating side effects.[7]

Two factors perpetuate worry and someone's emotional state: *heredity* (genetics) and *circumstances* (environment). Based on their hereditary makeup, some are predisposed to disruptive mental patterns. Others, on account of life circumstances, recurrently experience more stress than the average person.[8] As a health factor, someone's genetics remain mostly outside of one's control. Furthermore, while someone can choose how to respond to pressure, one has little control over the environmental influences contributing to stress. To mitigate mental angst, it behooves one to consider those aspects of life that are controllable.

The unfortunate alternative for many, when anxiety and mood get the better of us, is mental illness. About 25 percent of the world's population

---

6. Chandler, *Christian Spiritual Formation*, 108.
7. Davey, "Overprescribing Drugs."
8. Kendler and Prescott, *Genes, Environment, and Psychopathology*, 339–41.

will experience a mental disorder at some point. This number is higher in the United States (close to 50 percent).[9] The rediscovery of one's ancestral roots—integrally tied to emotional and relational wellness—is an aspect of identity one can gain control over. While a person's hereditary makeup and life circumstances reside mainly outside one's control, learning more about one's heritage is something anyone can proactively pursue.

Mental illness stems from an imbalance in the mind. However, body chemistry, on its own, only accounts for so much of this imbalance. I have accepted that I require some chemical supplement if I want to function best on a day-to-day basis. Still, not everyone has to take a pill to experience optimum health, and many would be remiss not to consider other social and behavioral sources impacting their mental health. It took me time to come to terms with the imbalance between the makings of our Italian American household and everyday life in twentieth-century US society. The forces of assimilation, imbedded in the makeup of the Western world, weighed on me as I found myself struggling to heed the apostle Paul's plea to "not conform" (Rom 12:2). For others, mental illness is tied to an imbalance in the pattern of their daily activities. People need structure in the amount of time spent between work, play, and rest.[10]

The individualism characterizing American society contrasts sharply with the family centeredness of Italians. The numerous state-sanctioned freedoms codified into the US Bill of Rights, although serving a purpose, tend to promote individualistic political ideals.[11] Society has a habit of "neutralizing" everyone in the name of tolerance and equality. Ethnicity is among those aspects of identity that Americans push aside in their public lives for the sake of equal treatment and common ground with those around them. The pursuit of equality seems a noble endeavor at face value. However, when striving after an ideal causes someone to distance oneself from qualities and behaviors integral to who a person is, one ends up forfeiting personal identity at the altar of a perceived public good. Alongside the rift concerning ethnic identity, many people experience a clash between the surrounding culture and their religious heritage. I, for example, have witnessed how the cynical, pragmatic modern mind can stymie the Pentecostal's jovial, faith-filled optimism. As feelings of social disconnect set in, they, in turn, can aggravate feelings of anxiety.

There is no doubt a physiological dimension to our well-being. Nevertheless, the human psyche remains something much more

9. World Health Organization, "Mental Disorders"; Cooley, "Mental Disorders," 863.
10. Leufstadius and Eklund, "Time Use," 53–63.
11. Chiu and Chen, "Individualism," 724.

complicated. We must take care for fear that we might reduce the human self to mere chemicals. The attempt to explain mental wellness merely in terms of neurotransmitters, synapses, and membrane receptors runs the risk of obscuring other sources of our mental health. Adopting a more *holistic* approach, one that also considers the social and lifestyle sources contributing to our mental health, helps us identify aspects of our lives we can actively improve.

LOOKING TO FAMILY FIRST

As crucial as a given prescription may be to one's physical and mental health, the process behind one's medical care remains more consequential. Without family-oriented treatment, medical care treads a slippery slope. For me, after all the medication experimented with, the sobering reality was that I ended up on the same prescription a sibling of mine had a positive experience with before I had even begun medical treatment. On my first visit to the psychiatrist, I was prescribed an SSRI and immediately began treatment. Sadly, the doctor never properly vetted me, handing me the prescription without inquiring about my family medical history. If efforts had been taken to determine family history upfront, I might have been spared years of experimentation with the various pill cocktails.

I was in my early twenties at the time and away at college. To be sure, I could have made a better effort to reach out to my family before signing on with the psychiatrist's prescription. Still, per proper medical practice, it is the clinician's responsibility to inquire with a patient upfront concerning their blood relatives' history of mental illness.[12] My admonishment to anyone, especially the young adult, is to ask your parents about your family's medical history before visiting a doctor (or at least before you start taking a pill).

Our medical history lends insight into the genetic factors determining the likelihood of illness. If a medication works for a sibling, someone who is made of the same raw chromosomal material as us, then there is a good chance it will benefit us. If experimentation is pursued, it should begin with a treatment option that has worked for a close blood relative. Although an unfortunate reality for many, overlooking family precedent in mental illness treatment is simply bad medicine. Years ago, the nature vs. nurture controversy threw speculation onto the *genetic* (nature-based) sources of mental illness, many turning to *environmental* (nurture-based) explanations instead. However, the relegation of nature-based approaches in this way no longer holds the same clout. Even if heredity is minimized

---

12. Doran, *Prescribing Mental Health Medication*, 30–31.

in mental illness treatment, unless siblings grew up in different homes from one another, family undeniably accounts for a shared environment. Our brother or sister was nurtured, more than anyone else, in surroundings similar to our own. The medical community increasingly recognizes the interworking of genetic and environmental factors in determining one's psychological makeup. Nevertheless, patients and psychiatrists ought to work together while prioritizing family medical history to diagnose and treat mental illness.[13]

In retrospect, I know that having the proper medication has contributed to my improved state of health. On the other hand, it is also clear that I must strive to uphold a family-oriented approach to medical care as much as it is within my power. This realization is more pertinent for me today as I have three children of my own. One or more of them will likely experience the same conditions I have suffered from, and I want them to have the best treatment experience possible. I will do my best to urge their doctors to prioritize medical care options based on family precedent before experimenting with other avenues.

The number of those seeking medical treatment for mental illness is on the rise. Between 1999 and 2014, for example, the number of those using antidepressants increased by 64 percent.[14] My advice to the one in two Americans who will experience mental illness at some point in their life, and those who know a loved one who has (that probably covers everyone), is to work diligently with the medical community to make family medical history a priority. It behooves families and educators alike to set a standard concerning the importance of family-based health care at an early age.

So while medicine has its value in treating our physical and mental conditions, perhaps more critical to our health is how medical care is conducted. A holistic approach to well-being is integrative of family-oriented medicine, alongside other lifestyle choices targeting our spiritual, emotional, and relational health.[15] The several faith- and family-based practices I have noted in this book—for example, the Sunday Sabbath, regular dinners, and siesta—have proved formative in my pursuit of a more holistic approach to well-being.

---

13. McGuffin and Katz, "Genes, Adversity, and Depression," 228–29; Goldhaber, *Nature-Nurture Debates*, 147–48.

14. Winerman, "By the Numbers," under "64%."

15. Chandler identifies the "spiritual, emotional, relational, intellectual, vocational, and resource formation dimensions" of wellness and personal formation (*Christian Spiritual Formation*, 277).

Reflection Questions:

- Do you ever find yourself caught in the vicious cycle of worry? How can rediscovering your ethnic and faith roots help you more fully comprehend why you think, feel, act (and worry) the way you do?
- While we cannot control our genetics and many of our circumstances, what are some areas of life we can manage? How can you actively promote your mental health by improving your social health, notably, your family relationships?
- Are you struggling with a physical or mental predicament? How might retracing your family history inform the way you and your doctors proceed with your treatment?

13

Finding Wholeness

For the Lord is good;
his steadfast love endures forever,
and his faithfulness to all generations.
—Psalm 100:5, NRSV

LOOKING BACK ON THE experiences of our forebears grants us a better appreciation for the personality traits, beliefs, and practices that define us today. In this chapter, I would like to revisit the central claim that rediscovering our ancestral roots (who we were *made to be*) adds purpose and meaning to our lives. The journey of rediscovery is a *theistic* one—exceeding *atheistic*, naturalistic assumptions about the evolution of the world and the *deistic* view that God wants nothing to do with creation. As illustrated in the previous chapter, unearthing our roots helps us manage change and stress and thus remains integral to a holistic approach to well-being. In light of my journey, I would like to take a closer look at how reincorporating specific activities and lifestyle choices ingrained in our faith and family heritage contributes to a fuller sense of wholeness and identity.

GOD'S CRAFTSMANSHIP AND PROVIDENCE IN OUR FAMILY HISTORY

In helping us see who we are *made to be*, rediscovering our roots points us beyond ourselves and even our ancestors to the character of a benevolent Maker. Moreover, faith assures us that our Maker is not stagnant and aloof, but a personal God who shaped us the way we are and has a splendid plan for each of our lives. The culture, ethnicity, and family we were born into are not the result of random forces or coincidence but are aspects of identity rooted in the blueprints of a loving God. Because someone crafted us, not haphazardly but with intentionality and care, as we unearth our roots, we can have confidence that our lives are inherently purposeful.

In *The Return of the King*, the third installment of J. R. R. Tolkien's tour de force, *The Lord of the Rings*, the warrior Aragorn is confronted with a choice—to embrace his roots or carry on in his present predicament. Aragorn was a "Ranger," belonging to a secretive, nomadic, and largely forgotten group who defended their lands in the "shadows." Rangers were loners and rarely engaged in more than petty battles. With the fate of Middle-earth hanging in the balance, the esteemed elf Lord Elrond approaches Aragorn. In Peter Jackson's movie adaptation of the book, Elrond implores Aragorn to take the reforged imperial sword, Andúril, claiming: "The man who can wield the power of this sword can summon to him an army more deadly than any that walks this earth. Put aside the ranger. Become who you were born to be."[1] The prospect of fulfilling who he was "born to be," implies Aragorn's life has always had a purpose. Even in embryonic form, his life had meaning, suggesting the transcendent deliberateness of a maker. Aragorn was of a royal bloodline, the rightful heir to the throne of Gondor. With impending war demanding that he rediscover and take up his place as king, when Elrond hands him the legendary sword, Aragorn unsheathes it, symbolizing the embrace of his inherited calling.

Like Aragorn, we are each created for a definite purpose. Consider that our family's welfare for generations to come (like the fate of Middle-earth) might rest on our reclaiming who we were born to be. When we consider our potential influence on generations well into the future, we can sense the gravitas attached to rediscovering our inherited calling. This journey might entail setting something aside as we start to see ourselves in a new light, even as Aragorn realized he was much more than a wandering Ranger. In embracing who he was made to be, Aragorn accepted that his life served a nobler end. Although I am a theist, I do not throw out evolutionary

---

1. Jackson, "*Andúril—Flame of the West.*"

theory with the bathwater, taking seriously those findings in geology and cosmology that point to an earth possibly much older than that supposed by traditional six-day creationism. The Genesis creation narrative contains metaphoric language better understood from the standpoint of *progressive creationism*. Accordingly, each creation "day" (Heb., *yom*) noted in chapters 2 and 3 of Genesis likely comprise an indefinite period, perhaps an entire age or eon. Such an interpretation permits an *old earth* view compatible with rock and fossil evidence, placing the earth at tens, if not hundreds, of millions of years old.[2]

I do not think it is contrary to the theistic worldview to imagine that God used something like modern science's "Big Bang" to bring the universe into existence. Nevertheless, I veer from those atheistic renderings that suggest that purely random, tangential forces caused this Big Bang. The theistic interpretation of the origin of the universe pivots on the principle of *creatio ex nihilo* (Lat. for "creation from nothing").[3] By postulating a creator, theism pivots on the craftsmanship and meaning behind all that exists.

The theistic approach to ancestry I have maintained in this book veers also from the diest's outlook. *Deism* flowered in Europe during the seventeenth and eighteenth centuries alongside the rise of the Enlightenment age in Western thought.[4] A quasi-religion, deism prevailed in an age of rationalism when human ingenuity was valued over the providence and watchful care of the Creator. For the deist, God created the world only to leave it to its own "natural" devices. Together with the theist, the deist concedes the *watchmaker* argument for God's existence. Indeed, the intricacy and craftsmanship embodied in the marvel of humanity point to a deliberate and wise Creator. On the other hand, while affirming that a supreme watchmaker designed and "wound up" the world, the deistic God would then leave the watch on someone's doorstep, never to see it again. A dynamically present and involved God is all too messy for the rationalist who imagines that only predetermined, natural causes carry out the course of history.

I invite the deist to consider that God is a personable being who is interested in and cares for the Creation he brought into form. To continue the watchmaker analogy, God not only winds the watch up but makes himself available should that watch one day need repair (and if you're like me, that's every day). Perhaps we are not ticking like we know we are supposed to. Still, there is hope. We are only a visit to the Watchmaker away

---

2. Hart, *Truth Aflame*, 171–72; Ross, *Matter of Days*, 23–24.
3. Craig, "Theism and Big Bang Cosmology," 218.
4. Livingstone, *Dictionary of the Christian Church*, 167.

from being restored to our original, God-intended form. We are never alone on the journey of rediscovery.

A theistic, faith-entranced approach to our ancestral roots means uncovering the handprint of God in our genealogy. As God's providence is underscored in the genealogies of Noah, Abraham, and Jesus, so the gaze of God's watchful eye, towards each generation of our family tree, is unremitting. God's craftsmanship and design in the world and universe beyond means that we had a purpose even before we were born. The rediscovery of God's purpose directs us to the character of the benevolent, loving, and faithful heavenly Father of all humankind.

USING LABELS CONSTRUCTIVELY

When misappropriated, labels are detrimental, pigeonholing us into various categories, roles, and classes. They can be particularly destructive when misused in the context of racial, ethnic, and religious identity. However, when applied in a meaningful way, labels have their merit. For instance, throughout this book, I have employed the terms "Italian," "American," and "Pentecostal" concerning my ancestral-identity. Conceptually, these specific descriptions help me grasp, discuss, and write about my family history. Many influences have contributed to my identity as an American. I grew up in the Northeast, where I attended public schools and had friendships with people from all walks of life. My love of sports, and basketball in particular—more popular in the US than anywhere else (and invented at a Massachusetts YMCA)—helped instill in me a vital sense of my Americanness from an early age. I never lived the rural life. And my faith ethos has always tilted more in the direction of integrationism than separatism. These factors have had a way of engaging me in the surrounding culture so that my Americanness has never been a point of contention.

On the other hand, I have had to work on reconnecting with my respective "Pentecostal" and "Italian" backgrounds. My college search for the baptism in the Spirit was, in large part, a quest to retrieve my faith heritage. Although an unforeseen result, the years I spent in a nondenominational church, and then in a Reformed context in college, likely muted some of what makes me Pentecostal (yet I remain grateful for each experience). My experience in the United Methodist Church over the last decade has helped me connect the dots with respect to this aspect of my heritage, as there is an inseparable link, historically-speaking, between Methodism and Pentecostalism. The late Pentecostal historian, Vinson Synan, regards the founder of Methodism, John Wesley, as the father of the

Pentecostal movement.[5] Early Methodism became a forerunner of several defining characteristics of Pentecostalism. In addition to emphasizing the experiential basis of religion, Wesley was an advocate of a Spirit-baptism-like experience.[6]

In recent years, I have begun to reintegrate facets of my Italian background, some attributes of which were more pronounced in my early years. Doing so has meant not just eating more spaghetti—although we have been more intentional about incorporating pasta into our weekly diet (my wife makes a mean pesto pasta dish!). I probably talk more with my hands now as well (another common Italian caricature), and useful when engaging a classroom audience. From play to work and rest, the rhythm of my life remains deeply colored by my identity as an Italian.

TAPPING INTO OUR ROOTS IN EVERYDAY LIFE

Looking to our roots helps us appreciate aspects of our personality and upbringing God always intended would shine through. The journey of rediscovery lends insight into concrete activities we can integrate to improve our lifestyle on a day-to-day basis. My wife and I have begun to place a firmer emphasis on family dinners and a Sabbath day of rest. While we have modified our Sunday dinner tradition to fit our current lifestyle—it is a bit more intimate (just the five of us), and we generally feast during the evening instead of the afternoon—we value this time together as we shift gears for the week ahead.

Another practice I have been more intentional about incorporating into my weekly routine is music. I played several instruments growing up, including the violin, piano, alto and baritone sax, the cello, and guitar. I was part of the school chorus, alongside singing roles in school and church plays. Whether my musicality draws more from my "Italian," "American," or "Pentecostal" roots is debatable. American symphonies and orchestras have a vibrant history. Furthermore, Pentecostals, even among Christian denominations, are known for their strong emphasis on music. The corporate singing and praise dimension of Pentecostal services rival the sermon in luster and intensity.

Certainly, when it comes to music, some credit goes to my Italian heritage. If one considers the impact Italians have had, not just on American

---

5. Synan, *Holiness-Pentecostal Tradition*, 1.

6. In his, *A Plain Account of Christian Perfection*, Wesley often speaks of a definitive post-conversion experience on par with the *subsequence* of Pentecostal Spirit baptism, identified variously as "pure love" or "entire sanctification" (*Plain Account*, 11:401–2).

music but on music culture worldwide—the opera, cantata, oratorio, sonata, concerto, and symphony (It., *sinfonia*) all originated in Italy—it is hard to deny the significance of music as a cultural marker of Italians.[7] Indeed, the introduction of dynamics into written music draws from Italian terminology: *pianissimo* (very soft), *mezzo piano* (medium soft), *forte* (loud), *crescendo* (getting louder), and *diminuendo* (getting softer). I recently picked up the guitar again. I joined the worship team at church and including weekly rehearsal practice throughout the week on my own. Both of my girls love to join in—Katarina has a toy piano and Teresa a toy guitar. We hope that their pretending to play now will become a passion for choosing an instrument of their own one day.

But we do not have to play an instrument to appreciate the value of music. Listening to music can tremendously influence our outlook on life. Our choice of music undoubtedly plays a role: heavy metal is probably not the best choice if the goal is soothing (although everyone has their preference). Songs of faith reach beyond the surface, cheering our hearts with joy and encouragement. Our local Christian radio station, K-Love, has alleviated many-a Monday morning blues for me. More recently, I have taken to Italian praise music to start off my days: this helps me find my center and pray while providing an outlet for learning the language of my forebears (I'm not fluent yet, though my Italian is improving). Perhaps in unearthing your roots, you also have been inspired to learn the songs and rhythms of your ancestors.

I have also been more intentional about incorporating the siesta (It., *riposa*) tradition into my day-to-day life. I have always enjoyed the occasional nap, especially as part of my Sabbath. Yet, today I am deliberate about carving out a midday break on most days of the week, generally beginning between noon and one. During this daily pause, I enjoy lunch while catching up on the daily news, and then some light reading and a short nap. Having this built-in break midday helps me cope with everyday stress. In taking a step back and removing myself from work, I gain needed perspective on daily pressures acting on my mind and body and return reinvigorated for the second half of the workday. While a siesta is particularly significant for Americans coming from countries that observe it, as illustrated in chapter 3, some rest midday has health benefits for everyone.

Reincorporating activities and traditions that connect us to our roots helps counterbalance modern society's stresses. Each of the practices I have discussed builds wellness differently. Dining regularly with family fosters social health. A daily dose of music (either playing or listening) contributes

---

7. Daniel, "History of Western Music," 558–59.

to a soulular kind of health. And the siesta reinforces bodily health. More of such practices (and, incidentally, less psychiatric medication) have given me greater overall contentment and stamina (and I'm sure if you asked my wife, she'd admit better performance in the bedroom as well!). While such practices may prove useful to others, I encourage each to build on the customs and traditions that resonate with their particular ancestral background. Cultivating specific faith-affirming ethnic practices ensures a sense of continuity and wholeness for ourselves and posterity.

Reflection Questions:

- Have you considered the meaning and intentionality which lie behind your family roots? How does understanding our experiences in light of who we were *made to be*, as creatures fashioned in the image of a loving heavenly father, inform the way we see ourselves and loved ones?
- Identify some labels (ethnic, religious, or cultural) that describe you. How can you apply these labels constructively to help you consider and discuss the ways your roots inform your life today?

Epilogue

As painted in the preceding pages, the rediscovery of my roots harkens to the legacy of a forgotten generation. I am reminded that my inheritance, both the challenges and successes, are intimately informed by the customs, beliefs, and pursuits of my migrant forebears. While no depiction of human history can escape the reality of fault or excess, my family history is mostly filled with trials overcome, hope, and exemplars to be championed and adored.

When we chart the path of rediscovery, building our tree and written (and perhaps pictorial) history, we will unearth stories that will enchant and cheer our hearts. On the other hand, we may uncover disconcerting truths, leading to discomfort, confusion, and even remorse. Nevertheless, we ought not to look at our roots as something "we can't escape." Even the less than desirable attributes about our forebears tell us something about their circumstances and the world they lived in generations, if not centuries, before our own. No matter how inspiring or bleak, each kernel we unearth offers an opportunity to learn and grow.

The path forward is to embrace our roots. We live in an increasingly depersonalized world that elevates the immediate now and performance over the many authentic experiences and people that shape who we are. It feels safer to abstract our identity and think only about today and getting by amid the present circumstances. The past is saturated with emotion, replete with ups and downs, heaps of adversity, and lingering failures. Still, how we think and feel in the present remains integrally tied to our history. Many of us would prefer to leave the past where it is and be rid of it. While we may be inclined to tuck away, ignore, or even reject our family heritage because of the pain and disappointments, this can lead to trivializing our roots, making it harder to face everyday challenges and insecurities. A "rootless" life is a troublesome path to tread in a world dictated by performance, the pressure to conform, and how others view us.[1]

The escalating depersonalization of Western society is exemplified in a mental health regiment built around what pills to take to remedy an apparent flaw in our biological makeup. We presume on the human psyche's complexity when we reduce distress, loneliness, fear, and insecurity to neurotransmitters and receptors. While holistic wellness should encompass the chemical dimensions of health, it should not be defined by them. Our chemistry is but a fraction of a wellness equation based on the sum of our experiences, past and present—especially our relational health.

Alongside depersonalization stands the twin foe of individualism. Pervading the Western mind is an emphasis on the individual over the collective. Success is measured by personal achievement, and the path to well-being dictated by whether we have tried the latest self-help technique. While self-advancement is an essential ingredient for any thriving society, a preoccupation with the self leads to shortsightedness and detachment. To tread this path is to ignore the social (relational) sources of who we are. Community-oriented solutions must temper our individual pursuits. When fully conceived, individualism leads to emotional *disconnect*, contributing to confusion about our identity and, potentially, any number of mental health predicaments.[2]

The role of the nuclear family continues to spiral downward among Americans. While this trend has had a pronounced effect on new immigrants, who are more susceptible to antisocial tendencies, the erosion of the family is something all Americans confront.[3] A renewed emphasis on who we are as relational beings—as members of specific communities, especially the family—is more essential now than ever. Rediscovering our roots helps us affirm the communal referent of our well-being, promising a way through the precarious waters of depersonalization and individualism.

It may take a personal crisis, as it did for me—a psychiatric diagnosis and life detour on an excessive amount of prescription medication—still, it's never too early to begin reconnecting with our roots. If there is any silver lining in the recent COVID-19 pandemic, it is that a global crisis has forced us to direct our attention to what's most important in life—family.

---

1. On the sting of failure and the performance trap, see Meyer, *Living Beyond Your Feelings*, 80–81.

2. M. Smith claims that biological psychology (emerging in the seventies) shifted the focus from social strategies to the individual, presaging the rise of the "narcissistic me" mentality and consumer-driven practices ("A Fine Balance," 9).

3. Berrol, *Growing Up American*, 102.

I consider now more than ever how precious my wife, Gabrielle, and three children, Joseph, Katarina, and Theresa, are to me, as well as my responsibility to do all in my power to look after them. Those experiencing loss and the breakdown of familiar routine during such a time, may find solace in an activity like building a family tree.

The reawakening of my Pentecostal heritage in recent years has helped me see why my everyday outlook is more mystical than most. I see better now why I value the experiential and supernatural more than the average modern mind. In retracing my ancestry's converging lines, I have begun to welcome those aspects of my personality that are distinctively American and uniquely Italian. I am a lover of American sports. I am built with the industrializing spirit undergirding the American work ethic. I watch mostly American movies and enjoy my share of American food. Yet, I am also very Italian. Not unlike all Americans, but many, I prefer and function best with a midday *riposa*. There is a distinct musical gene embedded in my personality: my fondness for classical music, the opera, and the piano admit a deep-seated Italian heritage.

Irrespective of class, nationality, and race, everyone can find new meaning by fortifying the bonds of family—where the journey of rediscovery begins. Strengthening our families means protecting mealtimes and planning outings and other lighthearted, stress-relief activities together. Along with the regular Sabbath, siesta, and a daily dose of music, building family-oriented practices into my life has improved my horizons.

The road of rediscovery says something significant about immigration. Looking at our family origins in the light of America's history, for example, should lead us to value our differences rather than belittle them. In a country built on the unique skills of a panoply of ethnic groups and sustained by the ready labor supply of new migrants, our future remains wrapped up in the fate of newcomers from distant lands. Immigration contributes to a healthy "intermixing" of cultures. By suffusing the many into one, the melting pot analogy overlooks the rich heterogeneity that makes the country's unity all the more astounding. Rather, the comingling of cultures elicits a grand and vibrant *mosaic*, more fortuitous than the image of many disparate elements melded into a metallic clump. The mosaic paradigm is more consistent with the biblical portrait of corporate identity. Indeed, eschatologically, the biblical outlook for the new creation is not a monolithic one but encompasses the many in their extraordinary diversity: "from every tribe and language and people and nation" (Rev 5:9, NRSV). Today, Americans are finding that it is not merely their neighborhoods that are becoming more ethnically diverse but also their families. The rise of the interracial family means that the traditional boundaries separating ethnic groups are becoming more permeable, promising innovative ways to approach ethnicity and race issues.[4]

Amid rapid societal change, awakened on the heels of advancements in industry, technology, travel, and medicine, rediscovering one's roots offers a vital sense of groundedness—a locus of continuity between the fluctuating present and the myriad of persons, places, and events comprising our past. Fast-forwarding a few decades from my youth, we have witnessed astronomical leaps in the fields of cybersecurity, chemical engineering, and genetics. Cloning and stem cell treatment were once only things we speculated about or watched in a sci-fi film. Unmanned drone crafts were exclusively a Star Wars phenomenon (now someone can purchase a camera drone from Best Buy for seventy-five bucks).

Change is inevitable. Even so, the tides of depersonalization and individualism are increasing at a rate that rivals such advancements. It is no wonder why the Ancestry corporation has created the craze it has today. Through resources accessible via Ancestry.com, many are employing advances in information technology to reconnect with something more crucial—the people who have shaped who we are. Genealogical databases like Ancestry.com are most beneficial when they help us restore ties and build new connections with immediate and extended family. The same Information Age that has distanced us from others through its obsession with handheld devices and immediate access, also affords specific resources. When used constructively, information technology complements the aim of rediscovering our roots.

I hope, upon reading this book, some will be persuaded to start their family tree (or return to one started years ago). Perhaps a family tree template provided on Ancestry.com or another database will be of use in this endeavor. However one chooses to proceed, the value of conversations with loved ones and sifting through family records (e.g., inherited writings and photos) cannot be overstated. Although there is no formula for rediscovering our roots, by constructively using the available means we set course on a journey that will reap rewards far beyond any tree diagram. In a world that reinforces individualism, retracing our roots offers an opportunity to have meaningful conversations and perhaps quality time with family members we haven't seen or talked to in years. We will stumble upon aunts, uncles, and cousins to whom we never knew we were related. This journey may lend new purpose to other forms of social media (e.g., Facebook or Myspace) as we use our networks to connect the dots of our lineage and forge new ties.

---

4. Mehta, *This Land Is Our Land*, 192–93.

Moreover, in reconnecting with others, we discover more about who we were *made to be*, and perhaps, more about our Maker. The One who fashioned us into being also wishes to see us through whatever predicament we presently face. Rediscovering my roots has been a journey of reconciliation. This journey consists of turning, from the things that keep me down towards my Creator; of bridging the person I am today with who I was made and always purposed to be; and buffering out the blemishes and grime to reveal someone created in the *imago Dei*. In the end, this journey will unveil more of the benevolent character of our heavenly Father. As we pursue this path, we will unravel lurking questions and begin to see ourselves in new ways. In turn, we will notice and perhaps reach out to others who, like ourselves, are yearning to learn more about who they are and from where they come.

Appendix A

How to Build Your Family History

BUILDING YOUR FAMILY HISTORY is a healthy exercise for anyone wishing to reconnect with your heritage. Perhaps you want to resolve the lurking questions about the *where*, *when*, and *who* of your roots. Well, you can start working on your family history anytime. There are two phases to building the history: *tracing* and *writing*. Tracing it entails research (drawing from family records, oral accounts, and genealogical databases) and creating your family tree. You can begin with just the names of your parents and grandparents and work from there. The next phase is writing out the history; this is something anyone can do. It does not need to be a full book-length account. Your written history can start with as little as a one-page sketch of significant markers in your ancestors' lives. If you have already done some research, tree-making, or writing on your family history years ago (independently or for a school project) you can pick up right where you left off.

To guide you in tracing the history and building your tree, you'll need to answer the foundational questions of *where*, *when*, and *who*. I have provided my family tree as an example as you fill in yours (see Appendix B). Once you have traced a portion of the history and have a working tree (it's okay if yours is not yet as detailed as mine), you are ready to start writing. You will find that the writing process itself will open up further insights to aid you in creating your tree and building the history (you may refer to chapter 5, focusing on the generation of my great-grandparents as an example for your written history). Begin with a generation you have substantial information on, starting with just a sentence or two about each ancestor of that generation. As you proceed with the writing, you will uncover vital nuggets about both previous and subsequent generations.

Any history is always a *working* history, informed and evolving as you encounter new morsels about the past and other "aha" moments in the present. It's okay if there are some gaps in the details at first. As a work in progress, the historical information you presently have on one ancestor may be considerably more detailed than that of another. In building my family history, I am ever eager to uncover new stories to fill in the gaps.

TRACING YOUR FAMILY HISTORY

When tracing your family history, define the scope of it upfront. I recommend beginning with a pedigree-style tree. A *pedigree* tree/chart traces the line of descent through parentage—including your parents, grandparents, great-grandparents, and so on (no siblings, aunts, uncles, or cousins). Decide how many generations you wish to chart. For instance, a *four-generational* tree reaches back to your great-grandparents—your generation counts first, followed by your parents, grandparents, and great-grandparents (the sample I provide in Appendix B is a *five-generational* model, reaching back to my great-great-grandparents).

A family pedigree supplies the main trunk and core branches of your tree. The essential information is comprised of *names*, *dates*, and *places*. The birth (and death) dates signal the time period each generation belongs to, while the birthplaces tell you where your family comes from (the foremost clue into your ethnicity). If subsequently you decide you wish to adapt it into an *extended* tree (with aunts, uncles, cousins, etc.), much of the pedigree's information will carry over. For example, although not always the case, there is a strong possibility the birthplace for your aunts and uncles will be the same as the birthplace of your respective parent.

The Sources for Your Family History

There are three main source types to draw from when building your family history: family records (e.g., inherited documents and pictures), personal conversations, and genealogical databases. I recommend beginning with the inherited materials.

Family Records

If your ancestors have left written testimonies and biographical accounts or photos behind, then locate these and start your history here. Perhaps you already have some of these filed away in your family archives at home. If your parents and/or grandparents are still living, follow up with them concerning their materials. Plan a visit to mine what they have in storage. Family photo albums can be a treasure trove of information, especially when they are annotated with key dates and places. Chances are if you broach your mom or grandma with questions about a family photo album, they will willingly walk you through it page by page. Be ready, with pad and pen in hand, because they're bound to load you with heaps of valuable nuggets about their life (as well as Uncle Bob and Cousin Jane!). Personal correspondences (between your ancestor and someone else) can also be a useful source of information. Other examples of items in a family archive: newspaper articles and obituaries, funeral programs, housing contracts, financial records, military discharge papers, wills, death/birth certificates, marriage licenses, baptismal certificates, confirmation records, and artifacts.

Oral Accounts

The second source type are oral accounts. Often, these emerge from our personal conversations with family members. After you have assessed family records, oral testimonies are crucial for filling in gaps left in your family profile. Casual chats over a meal or cup of coffee are an excellent place to begin. Suppose you are building a more extensive history. In that case, you may find it helpful to jot down details from your conversations or ask your loved ones whether you can record an informal interview with them (with an audio device or transcribing by hand). Conversations will often open the door to other sources. I recall more than a few discussions when midway through a cup of joe, a relative remembered about and invited to share another photo album or box of files.

Genealogical Databases

The last source type to consult is a genealogical database such as Ancestry.com. These are best used in conjunction with family records and oral accounts to fill in gaps in the details and corroborate the facts. Genealogical databases have the advantage of providing access to many official documents (birth and death certificates, marriage licenses, census data, military enlistment forms, etc.). The problem is that there is so much material. You are likely to become overwhelmed or lose the forest for the trees. Having some hard copy family records by your side will help make sense of the database information. Moreover, for a robust family history, you will want the subtleties of places, events, and times that only inherited materials and oral accounts afford.

While this book proposes a more personal approach built on family archives and conversations (supplemented by a genealogical database), some may wish to consult local library records. As someone who researches for a living, I encourage you to visit a library if you so choose. A subscription with a reliable online genealogical database will give you access to material you might discover at a local library; however, some will find perusing such records in hard-copy form helpful. With that said, don't prioritize the material found via an online database or local library above the personally-focused plan of action I have outlined. Precedent should be placed on family records and oral accounts.[1] A conversation over coffee, a thoughtful email, or a kindhearted phone call not only holds promise for building your tree but, moreover, can help to restore or erect new bridges with loved ones.

Creating Your Family Tree

Once you have defined your research scope and identified some sources, you're ready to create your family tree. It helps to start with just the basics—names (full and maiden) of your parents and grandparents—and work from there. As you move from a simple to a more in-depth tree, pencil in answers to the *who, when,* and *where* questions:

1. *Who?* Identify the relationships and names
2. *When?* Identify the key dates (birth, death, marriage, etc.)
3. *Where?* Identify the corresponding locations of birth, death, marriages, etc.

As you trace the history, I recommend beginning with the *who* question—concentrating on *relationships* and *names*. Start with your closest relatives (your parents) and reach back through the generations to your grandparents and great-grandparents, noting their full names (including maiden names if you have them).

After you have answered the *who* question to your liking, proceed to the *when* question—the key *dates*. Begin with the *birth* dates. You should have little trouble with your parents' birthdates but may need to do some digging for previous generations. Next, as best as you can, answer the *death* date for the ancestor. Then proceed to the *marriage* date. Marriage dates

---

1. Burroughs agrees concerning the priority of oral history and family documents (*Black Roots*, 80–107).

are integral to any family history as they indicate the point at which the respective branches of your tree merge. Be as specific as you wish (including day, month, and year). If a precise date for a given event cannot be determined, but you have narrowed it to plus or minus five years, feel free to approximate: signaled by the abbreviation *ca.* (from the Latin *circa* meaning "about") or just *abt.* (for "about"). You may also approximate the date using the abbreviations *bef.* (before) and *aft.* (after). For example, if you don't know the precise date of death, but know your ancestor must have lived beyond 1850, write "aft. 1850."

Once you are content with the key dates, proceed to the *places*, answering the corresponding *where* questions, especially: (1) Where was your ancestor born? (2) Where did they die? And (3) where were they married? When you have traced your history to this point (answering the essential questions concerning birth, death, and marriage), you will find that the corresponding dates and places coincide with other intriguing historical facts. Answering why your ancestor was born in such and such a place, for instance, may open the door to additional information about the prior generation (the ancestor's parentage). Examples of such questions include: Why were they living in a particular place? Or, what line of work were they in at the time? Differences in the city or country of birth from one generation to the next, or between birth and marriage locations, might be an indication that the family relocated or migrated during that timeframe. Relocation and emigration/immigration dates and places will lend valuable texture to your family history.

WRITING YOUR FAMILY HISTORY

Once you have traced your family history, sketching answers to the above questions and filling in your tree, you're ready to write the history. When writing it, move in the reverse direction: instead of beginning with your parents, move from previous to subsequent generations (i.e., start with the distant generation and move towards your own).

Depending on the available source material, I recommend beginning with your great-grandparents (a four-generational tree) or great-great-grandparents (a five-generational tree). The waters get murkier the further back you go. If you successfully write a four-generational history, a pat on the back is in order (make sure to give yourself due credit!). Afterward, you may decide to reach back and tack on another generation, which you may simply insert as a prequel chapter at the beginning of your history.

A Note on Photo Albums

Some may wish to structure the writing of their family history around photos. For those "visual" minds, a photo album or scrapbook-style family history can be very helpful. If you choose to go in this direction, be sure to annotate the pictures, at the least, with personal *names*, *places*, and *dates*. If in addition, you know the *occasion* for the picture, or a corresponding *story*, then write these in—such details will add vital texture to your history (see my photo assemblage at the end of chapter 5 for an example).

KEEP GOING!

As you trace and write your family history, you may find in a particular spot you are missing some key information. Don't get hung up on having to have in hand every name, date, and place before you can move on. If you are missing something, make a note to yourself and feel free to skip it, keep tracing and writing, and come back to it later. Remember, any history is a *work in progress*. Keep building, and don't get discouraged—enjoy the journey!

Appendix B

My Family Tree

146   APPENDIX B

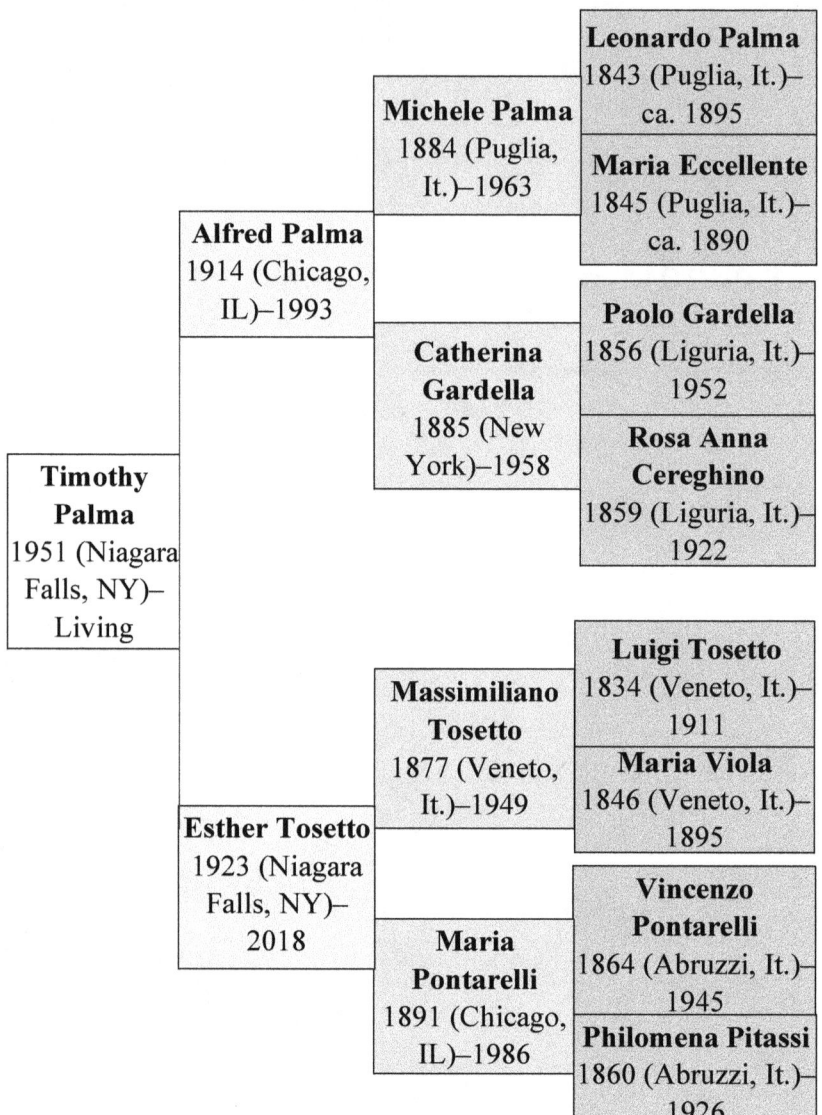

Figure Appendix B.1 Paternal Ancestry

APPENDIX B 147

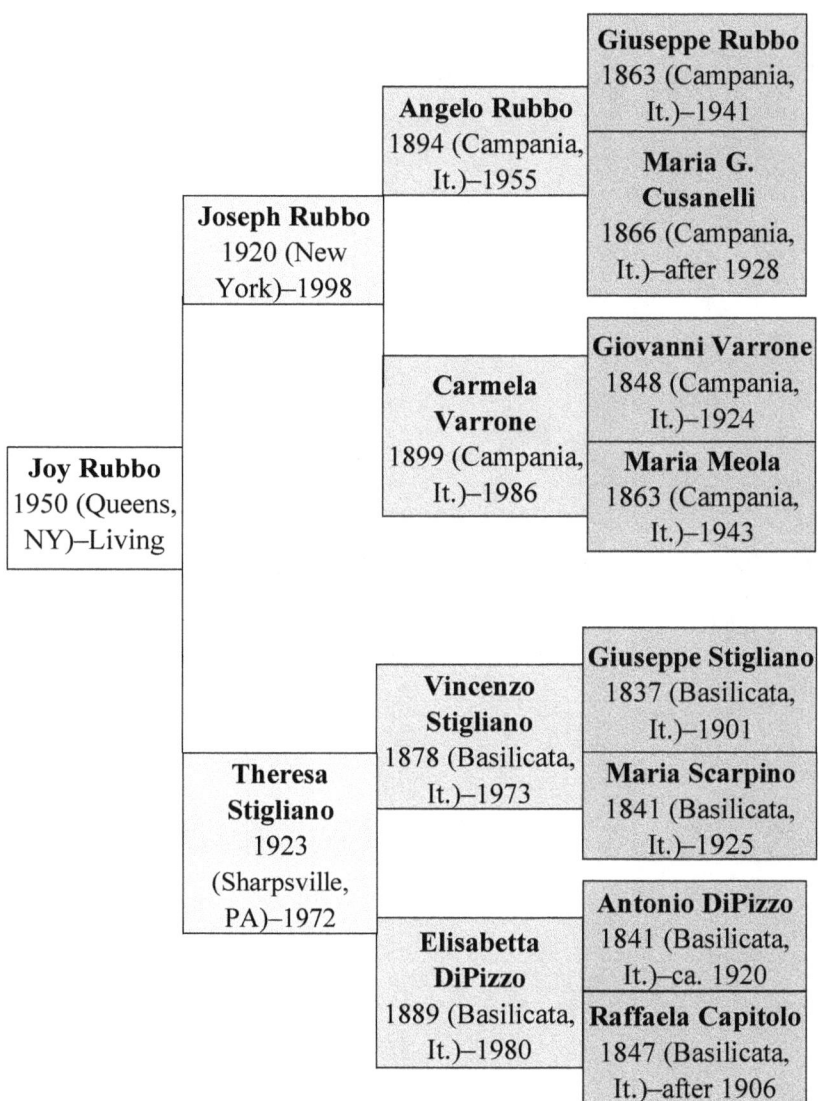

Figure Appendix B.2 Maternal Ancestry

Bibliography

"Ancestry Breaks November Sales Record." *Business Wire*, November 29, 2018. https://www.businesswire.com/news/home/20181129005208/en/Ancestry-Breaks-November-Sales-Record.
Ancestry.com. Lehi, UT, 2017. https://www.ancestry.com.
Anderson, Allan Heaton. *To the Ends of the Earth: Pentecostalism and the Transformation of Global Christianity*. Oxford: Oxford University Press, 2013.
Anderson, Robert M. *Vision of the Disinherited: The Making of American Pentecostalism*. Peabody, MA: Hendrickson, 1979.
Baily, Samuel L. *Immigrants in the Lands of Promise: Italians in Buenos Aires and New York City, 1870–1914*. Ithaca, NY: Cornell University Press, 2004.
Banfield, Edward C. *The Moral Basis of a Backward Society*. New York: Free Press, 1967.
Barrett, David B., and Todd M. Johnson. "Global Statistics." In the *New International Dictionary of Pentecostal and Charismatic Movements*, edited by Stanley M. Burgess, 284–302. Rev. ed. Grand Rapids: Zondervan, 2001.
Bartoş, Emil. "The Three Waves of Spiritual Renewal of the Pentecostal-Charismatic Movement." *Review of Ecumenical Studies Sibiu* 7, no. 1 (April 2015) 20–42. https://doi.org/10.1515/ress-2015-0003.
Beckwith, Francis. *David Hume's Argument Against Miracles: A Critical Analysis*. Lanham: University Press of America, 1989.
Berge, Jerica M., et al. "Similarities and Differences between Families Who Have Frequent and Infrequent Family Meals: A Qualitative Investigation of Low-Income and Minority Households." *Eating Behaviors* 29 (April 2018) 99–106.
Berrol, Selma Cantor. *Growing Up American: Immigrant Children in America Then and Now*. New York: Twayne, 1995.
Bew, Paul. *Ireland: The Politics of Enmity, 1789–2006*. Oxford: Oxford University Press, 2007.
Black, Edwin. *War Against the Weak: Eugenics and America's Campaign to Create a Master Race*. New York: Thunder's Mouth, 2003.
Blomberg, Craig L. *Jesus and the Gospels: An Introduction and Survey*. Nashville: B&H, 2009.

———. "Neither Hierarchicalist nor Egalitarian: Gender Roles in Paul." In *Paul and His Theology*, edited by Stanley E. Porter, 283–326. Boston: Brill Academic, 2005.

Bracco, Roberto. "Italy's Most Crucial Hour." *Pentecostal Evangel*, July 31, 1960, 2.

Bramblett, Reid. "Open Hours in Italy." Reidsitaly.com. Last updated January 2013. http://reidsitaly.com/planning/comm/open_hours.html.

Brindle, Ryan C., and Sarah M. Conklin. "Daytime Sleep Accelerates Cardiovascular Recovery after Psychological Stress." *International Journal of Behavioral Medicine* 19, no. 1 (March 2012) 111–14. https://doi.org/10.1007/s12529-011-9150-0.

Briscoe, Jill. "Does the Bible Really Say I Can't Teach Men?" *Christianity Today*, January 6, 2007. https://www.christianitytoday.com/women-leaders/2007/january/does-bible-really-say-i-cant-teach-men.html.

Brown, Mary Elizabeth. "Religion." In *The Italian American Experience: An Encyclopedia*, edited by Salvatore J. LaGumina, et al., 538–42. New York: Garland, 2000.

Buffurini-Guidi circolare. 9 April 1935, file 26, 299–1-C-Z, series PS G1. State Archives, Rome.

Bureau of Labor Statistics. "Women in the Labor Force: A Databook." April 2017. https://www.bls.gov/opub/reports/womens-databook/2016/home.htm.

———. "Women's Share of Labor Force to Edge Higher by 2008." February 14, 2000. https://www.bls.gov/opub/ted/2000/feb/wk3/art01.htm.

Burroughs, Tony. *Black Roots: A Beginners Guide to Tracing The African American Family Tree*. New York: Simon & Schuster, 2001.

Cai, M., et al. "Siesta is Associated with Reduced Systolic Blood Pressure Level and Decreased Prevalence of Hypertension in Older Adults." *Journal of Human Hypertension* 30, no. 3 (March 2016) 216–18. https://doi.org/10.1038/jhh.2015.70.

Cardozo, Arlene Rossen. *Jewish Family Celebrations: The Sabbath, Festivals, and Ceremonies*. New York: St. Martin's, 1982.

Cartledge, Mark J. *Charismatic Glossolalia: An Empirical-Theological Study*. Aldershot, UK: Ashgate, 2002.

Central Statistics Office. "Press Statement Census 2016 Results Profile 8—Irish Travelers, Ethnicity and Religion," October 12, 2017. https://www.cso.ie/en/csolatestnews/pressreleases/2017pressreleases/pressstatementcensus2016resultsprofile8-irishtravellersethnicityandreligion.

Chandler, Diane J. *Christian Spiritual Formation: An Integrated Approach for Personal and Relational Wholeness*. Downers Grove, IL: IVP Academic, 2014.

Chemnitz, Martin. *Examination of the Council of Trent: Part I*. St. Louis, MO: Concordia, 1971.

Chiu, Ming Ming, and Gaowei Chen. "Individualism." In *The Social History of the American Family: An Encyclopedia*, edited by Marilyn Coleman and Lawrence H. Ganong, 721–24. Los Angeles: SAGE, 2014. PDF e-book.

Cinotto, Simone. *The Italian American Table: Food, Family, and Community in New York City*. Urbana: University of Illinois Press, 2013.

Clark, Christine. "Genogram." In *Encyclopedia of Human Services and Diversity*, edited by Linwood H. Cousins, 584–86. Los Angeles: SAGE Reference, 2014.

Cohen, Jon S., and Francesco L. Galassi. "Sharecropping and Productivity: 'Feudal Residues' in Italian Agriculture, 1911." *The Economic History Review* 43 (November 1990) 646–56.

Cohen, Philip. "America Is Still a Patriarchy." *The Atlantic*, November 19, 2012. https://www.theatlantic.com/sexes/archive/2012/11/america-is-still-a-patriarchy/265428.
Cone, James H. *The Cross and the Lynching Tree*. Maryknoll, NY: Orbis, 2011.
"Conscription in the Kingdom of Italy." *NSindex*. Last updated April 27, 2019. https://nsindex.net/wiki/Conscription_in_the_Kingdom_of_Italy.
Cooley, Morgan E. "Mental Disorders." In *The Social History of the American Family: An Encyclopedia*, edited by Marilyn Coleman and Lawrence H. Ganong, 863–66. Los Angeles: SAGE, 2014. PDF e-book.
Craig, William Lane. "Theism and Big Bang Cosmology." In *Theism, Atheism, and Big Bang Cosmology*, by William Lane Craig and Quentin Smith, 218–31. Oxford: Oxford University Press, 1995.
Csizmadia, Annamaria. "Interracial Marriage." In *The Social History of the American Family: An Encyclopedia*, edited by Marilyn Coleman and Lawrence H. Ganong, 756–60. Los Angeles: SAGE, 2014. PDF e-book.
Cucchiari, Salvatore. "Between Shame and Sanctification: Patriarchy and Its Transformation in Sicilian Pentecostalism." *American Ethnologist* 17, no. 4 (1990) 687–707.
Cumbo, Enrico Carlson. "'As the Twig Is Bent, the Tree's Inclined': Growing up Italian in Toronto, 1905–1940." PhD diss., University of Toronto, 1996.
———. "'Your Old Men Will Dream Dreams': The Italian Pentecostal Experience in Canada, 1912–1945." *Journal of American Ethnic History* 19, no. 3 (2000) 47–48.
Daniel, Ralph Thomas. "The History of Western Music." In vol. 24 of the *New Encyclopaedia Britannica*, 553–64. 15th ed. Chicago: Encyclopaedia Britannica, 2007.
Darwin, Charles. *The Origin of Species*. Vol. 11 of *The Harvard Classics*. New York: P. F. Collier, 1909.
Davey, Graham C. L. "Overprescribing Drugs to Treat Mental Health Problems." *Psychology Today*, January 30, 2014. http://www.psychologytoday.com/blog/why-we-worry/201401/overprescribing-drugs-treat-mental-health-problems.
Davidson, Alan. *The Oxford Companion to Food*. Edited by Tom Jaine. 3rd ed. New York: Oxford University Press, 2014.
De Caro, Louis. *Our Heritage: The Christian Church of North America*. Sharon, PA: Christian Church of North America, 1977.
De Voragine, Jacobus. *The Golden Legend*. Translated by William Granger Ryan. Princeton, NJ: Princeton University Press, 2012.
Deaux, Kay, and Maykel Verkuyten. "The Social Psychology of Multiculturalism: Identity and Intergroup Relations." In *The Oxford Handbook of Multicultural Identity*, edited by Verónica Benet-Martínez and Ying-yi Hong, 118–38. Oxford: Oxford University Press, 2014.
Deno, Vivian. "God, Authority, and the Home: Gender, Race, and U.S. Pentecostals, 1900–1926." *Journal of Women's History* 16 (Fall 2004) 83–105.
DeSalvo, Louise. "Color: White/Complexion: Dark." In *Are Italians White?: How Race Is Made in America*, edited by Jennifer Guglielmo and Salvatore Salerno, 17–28. London: Routledge, 2003.
DiAngelo, Robin. *White Fragility: Why It's So Hard for White People to Talk About Racism*. Boston: Beacon, 2018.

Dinnerstein, Leonard. *Ethnic Americans: A History of Immigration*. New York: Columbia University Press, 1999.
Doran, Christopher M. *Prescribing Mental Health Medication: The Practitioner's Guide*. London: Routledge, 2013.
Doyle, Don H. "America's Garibaldi: The United States and Italian Unification." In *The Routledge History of Italian Americans*, edited by William J. Connell and Stanislao G. Pugliese, 69–90. New York: Routledge, 2018.
Drescher, Seymour. *Abolition: A History of Slavery and Antislavery*. Cambridge: Cambridge University Press, 2009.
Duffin, Jacalyn. *Medical Miracles: Doctors, Saints, and Healing in the Modern World*. Oxford: Oxford University Press, 2009.
Durasoff, Steve. *Bright Wind of the Spirit*. London: Hodder and Stoughton, 1972.
El-Zibdeh, Nour. "Understanding Muslim Fasting Practices." *Today's Dietitian*, August 2009. https://www.todaysdietitian.com/newarchives/072709p56.shtml.
Eliade, Mircea, and Charles J. Adams. *The Encyclopedia of Religion*. New York: Macmillan, 1987.
Emling, Shelley. *Setting the World on Fire: The Brief, Astonishing Life of St. Catherine of Siena*. New York: St. Martin's, 2016.
Espinosa, Gastón. "'Your Daughters Shall Prophesy': A History of Women in Ministry in the Latino Pentecostal Movement in the United States." In *Women and Twentieth-Century Protestantism*, edited by Margaret Lamberts Bendroth and Virginia Lieson Brereton, 25–48. Urbana: University of Illinois Press, 2002.
Fairall, H. H. *Italy Struggling into Light: Or, a Record of Prominent Events in its Civil, Religious, and Literary History*. Cincinnati, OH: Hitchcock and Walden, 1880.
Fee, Gordon D. *The First Epistle to the Corinthians*. Rev. ed. Grand Rapids: Eerdmans, 1987.
Ferrera, America. *American Like Me: Reflections on Life Between Cultures*. New York: Gallery, 2018.
Find a Grave. Lehi, UT, 2020. https://www.findagrave.com.
Flew, Antony. *A Dictionary of Philosophy*. New York: St. Martin's, 1980.
Foglio, Frank. *Hey God: Modern Miracles in the Lives of an Italian-American Family*. Plainfield, NJ: Logos International, 1972.
Fox, Maggie. "One in 6 Americans Take Antidepressants, Other Psychiatric Drugs." *NBC News*, December 12, 2016. https://www.nbcnews.com/health/health-news/one-6-americans-take-antidepressants-other-psychiatric-drugs-n695141.
Frieden, Bonnie. "'I Don't See Race': The Pitfalls of the Colorblind Mindset." *Washington University Political Review*, April 3, 2013. http://www.wupr.org/2013/04/03/%e2%80%9ci-don%e2%80%99t-see-race%e2%80%9d-the-pitfalls-of-the-colorblind-mindset/.
Gabaccia, Donna R. *Italy's Many Diasporas*. London: Routledge, 2000.
———. "Kinship, Culture, and Migration: A Sicilian Example." *Journal of American Ethnic History* 3 (Spring 1984) 39–53.
———. "Race, Nation, Hyphen: Italian-Americans and American Multiculturalism in Comparative Perspective." In *Are Italians White?: How Race Is Made in America*, edited by Jennifer Guglielmo and Salvatore Salerno, 44–59. London: Routledge, 2003.

Galvano, Stephen. "The Italian Christian Church, New York, New York." In *Fiftieth Anniversary: Christian Church of North America, 1927–1977*, edited by Stephen Galvano, 37. Sharon, PA: Christian Church of North America, 1977.

———. "Rev. Angelo Rubbo." In *Fiftieth Anniversary: Christian Church of North America, 1927–1977*, edited by Stephen Galvano, 36. Sharon, PA: Christian Church of North America, 1977.

Gans, Herbert J. "Boston's West End: An Urban Village." In *Divided Society: The Ethnic Experience in America*, edited by Colin Greer, 275–92. New York: Basic, 1974.

Garroni, Maria Susanna. "Interpreting Little Italies: Ethnicity as an Accident of Geography." In *The Routledge History of Italian Americans*, edited by William J. Connell and Stanislao G. Pugliese, 163–78. New York: Routledge, 2018.

Gensler, Harry J. *Ethics and the Golden Rule*. London: Routledge, 2013.

Giambastiani, Louis M. "In the Melting Pot: The Italians." *Extension* 7 (September 1912) 9–10.

Gibbons, Ann. "Shedding Light on Skin Color." *Science* 346 (November 2014) 934–36.

Giordano, Joe, and Monica McGoldrick. "Italian Families." In *Ethnicity and Family Therapy*, edited by Monica McGoldrick, et. al., 567–82. New York: Guilford, 1996.

Goldhaber, Dale. *The Nature-Nurture Debates: Bridging the Gap*. New York: Cambridge University Press, 2012.

Gramsci, Antonio. *Selections from Cultural Writings*. Translated and edited by Quentin Hoare and Geoffrey Nowell Smith. New York: International, 1985.

Groothuis, Douglas. *Truth Decay: Defending Christianity Against the Challenges of Postmodernism*. Downers Grove, IL: IVP, 2000.

Grudem, Wayne. *Systematic Theology*. Grand Rapids: Zondervan, 2000.

Guglielmo, Thomas A. *White on Arrival: Italians, Race, Color, and Power in Chicago, 1890–1945*. Oxford: Oxford University Press, 2003.

Handlin, Oscar. *The Uprooted: The Epic Story of the Great Migrations that Made the American People*. Boston: Little, Brown, 1951.

Harindranath, Ramaswami. *Perspectives on Global Cultures*. Berkshire, Eng.: Open University Press, 2006.

Hart, Larry D. *Truth Aflame: Theology for the Church in Renewal*. Grand Rapids: Zondervan, 2005.

Hersch, Joni, and Jennifer Bennett Shinall. "Fifty Years Later: The Legacy of the Civil Rights Act of 1964." *Journal of Policy Analysis and Management* 34, no. 2 (2015) 424–56.

Hess, Lisa M. "Befriending Outsiders: Table Fellowship, Habits of Mind, and Delight Amidst Difference." *Spiritus: A Journal of Christian Spirituality* 15, no. 1 (2015) 81–88.

Hoffman, David. *Italy: Little Known Facts About Well Known Places*. New York: Metro, 2008.

Hughson, Thomas. "Interpreting Vatican II: 'A New Pentecost.'" *Theological Studies* 69, no. 1 (February 2008) 3–37.

Hwang, Byung-tai. "Confucianism in Modernization: Comparative Study of China, Japan and Korea." PhD diss., University of California, Berkeley, 1979. https://search.proquest.com/docview/302913562.

Hyatt, Eddie L. *2000 Years of Charismatic Christianity: A Twenty-first Century Look at Church History from a Pentecostal/Charismatic Perspective*. Lake Mary, FL: Charisma, 2002.

Irvine, Jacqueline Jordan. "Lessons Learned: Implications for the Education of African Americans in Public Schools." In *Growing Up African American in Catholic Schools*, edited by Jacqueline Jordan Irvine and Michèle Foster, 170–76. New York: Teachers College, 1996.

Jackson, Jesse, Sr. "1984 Democratic National Convention Address, by Jesse Jackson, July 18, 1984." In *Voices of the African American Experience*, edited by Lionel C. Bascom, 574–81. Westport, CN: Greenwood, 2009. E-book.

Jackson, Peter. *The Lord of the Rings: The Return of the King*, special ed. DVD. Directed by Peter Jackson. Los Angeles: New Line Home Video, 2004.

Jastrow, Morris. *Hebrew and Babylonian Traditions*. London: Forgotten, 2012.

Jefferson, Thomas. "Notes on the State of Virginia." Query 14 in *Thomas Jefferson: Writings*, edited by Merrill D. Peterson, 268–69. New York: The Library of America, 1984.

John XXIII. "Pope John Convokes the Council." In *The Documents of Vatican II*. Edited by Walter M. Abbott, S.J. Translated by Joseph Gallagher, 703–9. London: Geoffrey Chapman, 1966.

Johnson, Todd M., et al. "Christianity 2012: The 200th Anniversary of American Foreign Missionaries." *International Bulletin of Missionary Research* 36 (January 2012) 28–29.

Kang, Huibin, et al. "The Siesta Habit is Associated with a Decreased Risk of Rupture of Intracranial Aneurysms." *Frontiers in Neurology* 8 (September 2017). https://doi.org/10.3389/fneur.2017.00451.

Karakaya, Sibel. "Bioavailability of Phenolic Compounds." *Critical Reviews in Food Science and Nutrition; Boca Raton* 44, no. 6 (2004) 453–64.

Keener, Craig S. *1–2 Corinthians*. Cambridge: Cambridge University Press, 2005.

Kendler, Kenneth S., and Carol A. Prescott. *Genes, Environment, and Psychopathology*. New York: Guilford, 2006.

Ketcham, Ralph. *Individualism and Public Life: A Modern Dilemma*. New York: Basil Blackwell, 1987.

Keys, Scott. "Immigration Act of 1965." In vol. 1 of *Encyclopedia of Immigration and Migration in the American West*, edited by Gordon Morris Bakken and Alexandra Kindell, 315–16. London: Sage Publications, 2012.

Kidder, Rushworth M. *How Good People Make Tough Choices*. New York: Quill, 2003.

Krul, Arno J., et al. "Self-Reported and Measured Weight, Height and Body Mass Index (BMI) in Italy, the Netherlands and North America." *The European Journal of Public Health* 21, no. 4 (August 2011) 414–19.

Kte'pi, Bill. "Social History of American Families: 2001 to the Present." In *The Social History of the American Family: An Encyclopedia*, edited by Marilyn Coleman and Lawrence H. Ganong, 1240–43. Los Angeles: SAGE, 2014.

Lane, Tony. *A Concise History of Christian Thought*. Rev. ed. Grand Rapids: Baker Academic, 2006.

Lee-Barnewall, Michelle. *Neither Complementarian nor Egalitarian: A Kingdom Corrective to the Evangelical Gender Debate*. Grand Rapids: Baker Academic, 2016.

Leufstadius, Christel, and Mona Eklund. "Time Use among Individuals with Persistent Mental Illness: Identifying Risk Factors for Imbalance in Daily Activities." *Scandinavian Journal of Occupational Therapy* 21 (September 2014) 53–63. https://doi.org/10.3109/11038128.2014.952905.

Livingston, Gretchen. "The Changing Profile of Unmarried Parents." *Pew Research Center*, April 25, 2018. https://www.pewsocialtrends.org/2018/04/25/the-changing-profile-of-unmarried-parents.

Livingstone, E. A. *The Concise Oxford Dictionary of the Christian Church*. Rev. ed. Oxford: Oxford University Press, 2006.

Loos, J. "Syracuse's Foreign Born Population—Some Statistics." *Syracuse Sunday Herald*, March 19, 1897, 28.

Mangione, Jerre, and Ben Morreale. *La storia: Five Centuries of the Italian American Experience*. New York: HarperCollins, 1992.

Manji, Irshad. *Don't Label Me: An Incredible Conversation for Divided Times*. New York: St. Martin's, 2019.

Martin, Elizabeth, and Robert Hine, eds. *A Dictionary of Biology*. Rev. ed. New York: Oxford University Press, 2015. http://www.oxfordreference.com/view/10.1093/acref/9780198714378.001.0001/acref-9780198714378-e-4040.

Mazzocco, Philip J. *The Psychology of Racial Colorblindness*. New York: Palgrave, 2017.

McDonough, William K. *The Divine Family: The Trinity and Our Life in God*. Cincinnati, OH: St. Antony Messenger, 2005.

McGuffin, Peter, and Randy Katz. "Genes, Adversity, and Depression." In *Nature, Nurture, and Psychology*, edited by Robert Plomin and Gerald E. MacClearn, 217–30. Washington, DC: American Psychological Association, 1996.

McPherson, James M. *The War That Forged a Nation: Why the Civil War Still Matters*. Oxford: Oxford University Press, 2015.

Medina, Néstor. *Mestizaje: (Re)Mapping Race, Culture, and Faith in Latina/o Catholicism*. Maryknoll, NY: Orbis, 2009.

Mehra, Nishta J. *Brown White Black: An American Family at the Intersection of Race, Gender, Sexuality, and Religion*. New York: Picador, 2019.

Mehta, Suketu. *This Land Is Our Land: An Immigrant's Manifesto*. New York: Farrar, Straus, and Giroux, 2019.

Mekonnen, Alemayehu. *The West and China in Africa: Civilization without Justice*. Eugene, OR: Wipf and Stock, 2015.

Meyer, Joyce. *Living Beyond Your Feelings: Controlling Emotions So They Don't Control You*. New York: FaithWords, 2011.

Miller, Pavla. "Demography and Gender Regimes: The Case of Italians and Ethnic Traditions." *Journal of Population Research* 21, no. 2 (2004) 199–222.

Murray, Abdu. *Saving Truth: Finding Meaning & Clarity in a Post-Truth World*. Grand Rapids: Zondervan, 2018.

Musmanno, Michael A. *The Story of the Italians in America*. Garden City, NY: Doubleday, 1965.

National Academies of Sciences, Engineering, and Medicine. *The Integration of Immigrants into American Society*. Washington, DC: National Academies, 2015.

Nelli, Humbert S. *Italians in Chicago: A Study in Ethnic Mobility*. New York: Oxford University Press, 1970.

Neumark-Sztainer, Dianne, et al. "Changes in the Frequency of Family Meals From 1999 to 2010 in the Homes of Adolescents: Trends by Sociodemographic Characteristics." *Journal of Adolescent Health* 52, no. 2 (2013) 201–6.

Noffke, Suzanne. "Introduction." In *Catherine of Siena: The Dialogue*. Translated by Suzanne Noffke. New York: Paulist, 1980.

Northern Ireland Statistics and Research Agency. "Census 2011: Key Statistics for Northern Ireland." December 2012. https://www.nisra.gov.uk/sites/nisra.gov.uk/files/publications/2011-census-results-key-statistics-northern-ireland-report-11-december-2012.pdf.

Orsi, Robert A. *The Madonna of 115th Street: Faith and Community in Italian Harlem, 1880–1950.* New Haven, CT: Yale University Press, 1985.

Palma, Alfred. "A Cloud of Witnesses: Two Unforgettable Pioneers of the Niagara Mohawk District." In *Fiftieth Anniversary: Christian Church of North America, 1927–1977,* edited by Stephen Galvano, 35. Sharon, PA: Christian Church of North America, 1977.

———. "Maximillian Tosetto." Syracuse, NY: privately printed, 1972.

———. "Michael Palma." In *Fiftieth Anniversary: Christian Church of North America, 1927–1977,* edited by Stephen Galvano, 34. Sharon, PA: Christian Church of North America, 1977.

Palma, Kathryn. "Final Tribute to M. Tosetto." *Lighthouse,* October 1949, 6.

Palma, Michael, and Kathryn Palma, eds. *Nuovo libro d'inni e salmi spirituali.* Pittsburgh, PA: Missionary Society of the Christian Church of North America, 1959.

Palma, Paul J. "Between Abstention and Moderation: The Example of the Jerusalem Council and the Italian Pentecostal Holiness Ethic." *Journal of the European Pentecostal Theological Association* 39, no. 1 (January 2, 2019) 14–24.

———. *Italian American Pentecostalism and the Struggle for Religious Identity.* New York: Routledge, 2019.

———. "Maximillian Tosetto." In the *Encyclopedia of Christianity in the United States,* edited by George Thomas Kurian and Mark A. Lamport, 2318–19. Lanham, MD: Rowman & Littlefield, 2016.

Paraskakis, Emmanouil, et al. "Siesta and Sleep Patterns in a Sample of Adolescents in Greece." *Pediatrics International* 50, no. 5 (2008) 690–93. https://doi.org/10.1111/j.1442-200X.2008.02632.x.

Parham, Charles F. *A Voice Crying in the Wilderness.* Kansas City, MO: privately published, 1902.

Paul VI. "Gaudete in domino." May 9, 1975. http://www.vatican.va/holy_father/paul_vi/apost_exhortations/documents/hf_p-vi_exh_19750509_gaudete-in-domino_en.html.

Perez, Anthony Daniel, and Charles Hirschman. "The Changing Racial and Ethnic Composition of the US Population: Emerging American Identities." *Population and Development Review* 35, no. 1 (March 2009) 1–51.

Peters, Jeffrey. "Modelo Is Fighting for Honor." *News and Times* (blog), June 21, 2017. https://www.newsandtimes.com/2017/06/modelo-is-fighting-for-honor.

Piper, John. *A Hunger for God: Desiring God Through Fasting and Prayer.* Wheaton, IL: Crossway, 1997.

Pitrè, Giuseppe. *Proverbi Siciliani: volume primo.* Vol. 8 of *Biblioteca delle tradizioni popolari Siciliane.* Palermo: Luigi Pedone Lauriel, 1880.

Recinos, Harold J. *Hear the Cry: A Latino Pastor Challenges the Church.* Louisville, KY: Westminster/John Knox, 1989.

Riccio, Anthony V. *Portrait of an Italian-American Neighborhood: The North End of Boston.* New York: Center for Migration Studies, 1998.

Riis, Jacob A. *How the Other Half Lives: Studies among the Tenements of New York.* New York: Dover, 1971.

Robeck, Cecil M., Jr. *The Azusa Street Mission and Revival: The Birth of the Global Pentecostal Movement*. Nashville: Thomas Nelson, 2006.

———. "William J. Seymour and 'the Bible Evidence.'" In *Initial Evidence: Historical and Biblical Perspectives on the Pentecostal Doctrine of Spirit Baptism*, edited by Gary B. McGee, 72–95. Peabody, MA: Hendrickson, 1991.

Ross, Hugh. *The Creator and the Cosmos: How the Latest Scientific Discoveries Reveal God*. Rev. ed. Covina, CA: Reasons to Believe, 2018.

———. *A Matter of Days: Resolving a Creation Controversy*. Rev. ed. Colorado Springs, CO: NavPress, 2015.

Rotbart, Harley A. *Miracles We Have Seen: America's Leading Physicians Share Stories They Can't Forget*. Deerfield Beach, FL: Health Communications, 2016.

Rubbo, Joseph. "A Brief History of the Christian Church of Bayside." In the *Twenty-Fifth Anniversary: Christian Church of Bayside*. Bayside, NY: privately printed, 1979.

Russell, Cheryl. *The Master Trend: How the Baby Boom Generation Is Remaking America*. Boston: Springer, 2013.

Saggio, Joseph J. "Native American Christian Higher Education: Challenges and Opportunities for the 21st Century." *Christian Higher Education* 3, no. 4 (October 2004) 329–47.

Sailhamer, John H. *The Pentateuch as Narrative: A Biblical-Theological Commentary*. Grand Rapids: Zondervan, 1992.

Sarna, Jonathan D. *American Judaism: A History*. New Haven, CT: Yale University Press, 2005.

Sartorio, Enrico C. *Social and Religious Life of Italians in America*. Clifton, NJ: Augustus M. Kelley, 1974.

Schramm, David G., and G. E. Kawika Allen. "Divorce and Religion." In *The Social History of the American Family: An Encyclopedia*, edited by Marilyn Coleman and Lawrence H. Ganong, 365–68. Los Angeles: SAGE, 2014. PDF e-book.

Schroth, Stephen T. "Child Abuse." In *The Social History of the American Family: An Encyclopedia*, edited by Marilyn Coleman and Lawrence H. Ganong, 178–81. Los Angeles: SAGE, 2014. PDF e-book.

Schwartz, Seth J., et al. "The Identity Dynamics of Acculturation and Multiculturalism: Situating Acculturation in Context." In *The Oxford Handbook of Multicultural Identity*, edited by Verónica Benet-Martínez and Ying-yi Hong, 57–93. Oxford: Oxford University Press, 2014.

Settles, Isis H., and Nicole T. Buchanan. "Multiple Groups, Multiple Identities, and Intersectionality." In *The Oxford Handbook of Multicultural Identity*, edited by Verónica Benet-Martínez and Ying-yi Hong, 165–66. Oxford: Oxford University Press, 2014.

Shapiro, Paul, dir. "Episode 10:00 PM–11:00 PM." In *24: Season One*, created by Joel Surnow and Robert Cochran, special ed. DVD. Beverly Hills, CA: Twentieth Century Fox Home Entertainment, 2008.

Shriver, William Payne. *Adventure in Missions: The Story of Presbyterian Work with Italians*. New York: Board of National Missions of the Presbyterian Church in the USA, 1946.

Simon, Rita J., and Mohamed Alaa Abdel-Moneim. *A Handbook of Military Conscription and Composition the World Over*. Lanham, MD: Lexington, 2011.

Smith, Denis Mack. *Modern Italy: A Political History*. Ann Arbor: University of Michigan Press, 1997.

Smith, Matthew. "A Fine Balance: Individualism, Society and the Prevention of Mental Illness in the United States, 1945–1968." *Palgrave Communications* 2, no. 1 (December 2016) 1–11. http://dx.doi.org.ezproxy.regent.edu/10.1057/palcomms.2016.24.

Smokowski, Paul R., et al. "Ethnic Identity and Mental Health in American Indian Youth: Examining Mediation Pathways Through Self-Esteem, and Future Optimism." *Journal of Youth and Adolescence* 43, no. 3 (March 2014) 343–55.

Southern Baptist Convention. "Baptist Faith and Message 2000." SBC.net. http://www.sbc.net/bfm2000/bfm2000.asp.

Sowell, Thomas. *Ethnic America: A History*. New York: Basic, 1981.

Spencer, Herbert. *The Principles of Biology*. London: William and Norgate, 1864.

Spickard, Paul R. *Almost All Aliens*. New York: Routledge, 2007.

Spooner, W. A. "Golden Rule." In vol. 6 of the *Encyclopedia of Religion and Ethics*, edited by James Hastings, 310–12. New York: Charles Scribner's Sons, 1917.

Stigliano, Dominick. *The Stigliano Story*. Niles, OH: Krok Printing, 1998.

Stigliano, Esther. Interview with the author. July 16, 2016. Audio recording, personal files of Paul J. Palma, Hampton, VA.

Stone, Linda, and Diane E. King. *Kinship and Gender: An Introduction*. Rev. ed. New York: Routledge, 2018.

Storms, Sam. *The Beginner's Guide to Spiritual Gifts*. Ann Arbor, MI: Vine, 2002.

Strong, James. *Dictionary of the Hebrew Bible*. In *Strong's Exhaustive Concordance*. Nashville: Crusade Bible, 1960.

Synan, Vinson. *The Holiness-Pentecostal Tradition: Charismatic Movements in the Twentieth Century*. Grand Rapids: Eerdmans, 1997.

Taylor, Paul. "Nap Time." *Pew Research Center*, July 29, 2009. https://www.pewsocialtrends.org/2009/07/29/nap-time.

Thandeka. *Learning to Be White: Money, Race, and God in America*. New York: Continuum, 1999.

Thurston, Herbert. "Kiss." *The Catholic Encyclopedia*. Vol. 8. New York: Robert Appleton, 1910. http://www.newadvent.org/cathen/08663a.htm.

Tirabassi, Maddalena. "Why Italians Left Italy: The Physics and Politics of Migration, 1870–1920." In *The Routledge History of Italian Americans*, edited by William J. Connell and Stanislao G. Pugliese, 117–31. New York: Routledge, 2018.

Tiscareño-Sato, Graciela. "Our American Dream: Meet the First Latina US Military Pilot." *Fox News*, May 28, 2012. https://www.foxnews.com/world/our-american-dream-meet-the-first-latina-us-military-pilot.

Toppi, Francesco. *E mi sarete testimoni: Il movimento Pentecostale e le Assemblee di Dio in Italia*. Rome: ADI Media, 1999.

———. *Massimiliano Tosetto*. I pionieri del risveglio Pentecostale Italiano serie. Rome: ADI-Media, 1998.

Tosetto, Maria. Interview by Peter Vodola (Maria's grandson). March 1978. Transcript, personal files of Paul J. Palma, Hampton, VA.

US Census Bureau. "American Community Survey: Five-Year Data Profile." 2018. https://www.census.gov/acs/www/data/data-tables-and-tools/data-profiles/2018.

———. *Religious Bodies: 1936*. Vol. 2. Pt. 1. Washington, DC: US Government Printing Office, 1941.

———. *Statistical Abstract of the United States: 1991*. Washington, DC: US Government Printing Office, 1991.

Vecoli, Rudolph J. "Contadini in Chicago: A Critique of The Uprooted." *The Journal of American History* 51, no. 3 (December 1964) 404–17.

———. "Prelates and Peasants: Italian Immigrants and the Catholic Church." *Journal of Social History* 2 (April 1969) 217–68.

Vondey, Wolfgang. "Does God Have a Place in the Universe? Physics and the Quest for the Holy Spirit." In *Science and the Spirit: A Pentecostal Engagement with the Sciences*, edited by James K. A. Smith and Amos Yong, 75–91. Bloomington: Indiana University Press, 2010.

Warrington, Keith. *Pentecostal Theology: A Theology of Encounter*. London: T&T Clark, 2008.

Wesley, John. *A Plain Account of Christian Perfection*. In *The Works of John Wesley*. Grand Rapids: Zondervan, 1958.

Whitaker, Robert. *Mad in America: Bad Science, Bad Medicine, and the Enduring Mistreatment of the Mentally Ill*. 2nd ed. New York: Basic, 2010.

Widdowson, Mark. "Avoidance, Vicious Cycles, and Experiential Disconfirmation of Script: Two New Theoretical Concepts and One Mechanism of Change in the Psychotherapy of Depression and Anxiety." *Transactional Analysis Journal; Thousand Oaks* 44, no. 3 (July 2014) 194–207. http://dx.doi.org.ezproxy.regent.edu:2048/10.1177/0362153714554207.

Wilken, Robert Louis. *The First Thousand Years: A Global History of Christianity*. New Haven, CT: Yale University Press, 2012.

Williams, George H., and Edith Waldvogel. "A History of Speaking in Tongues and Related Gifts." In *The Charismatic Movement*, edited by Michael P. Hamilton, 61–113. Grand Rapids: Eerdmans, 1975.

Williams, J. Rodman. *Renewal Theology: Systematic Theology from a Charismatic Perspective*. Grand Rapids: Zondervan, 1996. PDF e-book.

Winerman, Lea. "By the Numbers: Antidepressant Use on the Rise." *Monitor on Psychology* 48, no. 10 (November 2017). https://www.apa.org/monitor/2017/11/numbers.

World Health Organization. "Mental Disorders Affect One in Four People." October 4, 2001. https://www.who.int/whr/2001/media_centre/press_release/en.

Wright, Daryn. "The Longest Lunch Breaks Around the World." *Saveur*, November 18, 2016. https://www.saveur.com/longest-lunch-breaks-around-world.

Wright, N. T. "The Biblical Basis for Women's Service in the Church." *Priscilla Papers* 20, no. 4 (2006) 5–10.

Yong, Amos. *The Future of Evangelical Theology: Soundings from the Asian American Diaspora*. Downers Grove, IL: IVP, 2014.

———. *The Spirit of Creation: Modern Science and Divine Action in the Pentecostal-Charismatic Imagination*. Grand Rapids: Eerdmans, 2011.

Zangwill, Israel. *The Melting-Pot: Drama in Four Acts*. New York: Macmillan, 1916.

Zucchi, John E. *Italians in Toronto: Development of a National Identity, 1875–1935*. Kingston, ON: McGill-Queens University Press, 1988.

Zylstra, Sarah Eekhoff. "Pope Francis Apologizes for Pentecostal Persecution, But Italy's Evangelicals Remain Wary." *Christianity Today*, July 30, 2014. https://www.christianitytoday.com/news/2014/july/pope-francis-apologizes-for-pentecostal-persecution-italy.html.

Subject Index

Abraham (Abram) 5–6, 129
Abruzzi 48, 76
Africa, African 44, 70–72, 74, 75
African Americans 36, 69n17, 71–72, 74, 88
agrarian lifestyle
    contadini and Africans and 70–71
    in Italy 21, 43, 54, 60–62, 76; *see also* subsistent lifestyle
agricultural crisis, European 61, 83
"amoral familism" 105–6
ancestral-identity 4, 7, 35–36, 39, 117, 120, 129
Ancestry.com 5, 36, 136, 141
anti-organizationalism 85
Aquinas, Thomas 86
Asian Americans 36, 79–80
Assemblea Cristiana (Christian Assembly) 46, 48, 84–85
Assemblies of God 92, 115; Italian 84
assimilation 2, 4, 25, 122
atheist, atheistic 79, 126, 128
Austro-Hungarians 44
Azusa Street revival 78

Banfield, Edward C. 105–6
baptism, Spirit 48, 86, 92, 95, 129, 130, 130n6
baptism, water 46

Baptist Church, Baptists 47, 76, 86n21, 91, 115, 115n11
Basilicata 51, 76
Beckwith, Francis J. 90
Big Bang theory 128
Black Codes 68
Bonaventure 86
British Abolition Bill 70
Buddhism 2, 63
Buffarini Guidi circular 87

Calabria 59
Campania 50, 59, 76, 88
Cardozo, Arlene Rossen 109
Catherine of Siena 86, 95
Catholic Church, Catholics, Catholicism
    in America 81, 83, 84, 88, 91
    Charismatic renewal and 87
    excommunication from 85, 91
    folk-religion and 83–84, 86, 86n21
    Irish and 1–2, 66–67
    in Italy 2, 47–48, 50, 80–83
    mystical tradition of 83, 86, 95
    strictures of 85–86; *see also* Second Vatican Council
Chandler, Diane 121, 124n15
Charismatic *see under* renewal, renewalist
Chicago 23, 45–46, 47–48, 78, 84–85
China, Chinese 31, 44, 63, 75, 79

SUBJECT INDEX

Christian Church of North America (CCNA, International Fellowship of Christian Assemblies) 23, 46, 78, 78n1 81–82, 115
Cinotto, Simone 108
Citizenship (naturalization), American 22, 53, 73
Civil Rights Act (of 1964) 76
civil rights movement 74–75, 76
Civil War 68
collectivist, collectivism 35, 39, 80
colonialism, British 70
Columbus, Christopher 44
Confucius, Confucian philosophy 63, 79–80
conscription, military 51–52
consumerism 2, 134n2
contadini (peasants) 21–22, 43, 60–61, 71, 80–81, 83–85, 88, 106; *see also* Italy, Italian
Council of Trent, Tridentine 86n22, 88
culture, cultures
    acculturation 4, 21, 31, 67
    contemporary xiii, 25–26, 30, 80, 98, 110
    ethnocultural 83, 88
    Italian 13, 60, 101, 104–7, 113, 131
    multicultural (diversity of) 2, 5, 7, 36, 76, 135
    popular (pop) 36, 102, 107; *see also* food culture; Western society (culture)
Crawford, Florence 114
creation, theology of
    creatio ex nihilo 128
    God's character and 5–6, 75, 97, 114
    new creation 135
    progressive creationism 128
Cuba, Cuban 44
Cucchiari, Salvatore 113
Custodio, Olga 34

Darwin, Charles 71, 73; *see also* social Darwinism
David, King 6, 24
deist, deism 5, 126, 128
DiAngelo, Robin 74–75

diet 26, 108, 130
dietary laws 109
dominant-subaltern critical theory 70
Duffin, Jacalyn 97

East Asian 2, 63, 79; *see also* China, Chinese; Japan, Japanese
Eastern Orthodox 87
economy, economic 2, 4, 47, 59, 62, 66, 68, 71, 83, 105, 108
Edict of Thessalonica 81
egalitarianism, egalitarian 113–16
emotion, emotionality 37, 73, 84, 121–22, 124, 133, 134
Emperor Theodosius I 81
England, English 44, 71
ethnicity 22, 24, 65, 70, 77, 122, 127, 136, 140
ethnocentrism, ethnocentric 24–26
extended (*parenti*) family 53, 54, 60, 104, 106, 110, 136

faith-entranced approach xv, 4, 129
family, erosion of 4, 101, 134
family dynamics 37, 113
family history
    medical 123–24
    records and oral accounts regarding 120, 136, 139–42
family tree
    building of 54, 76, 80, 120, 129, 135, 136, 139, 142–43
    pedigree vs. *extended* model of 140
fascism 71, 87
Ferrera, America 25
festa, feste 52, 83–84
feudalism, feudal 60
food culture 3, 17, 33–34, 108–9
France 30
Francis of Assisi 86
Francis, Pope 88
French Americans 26, 30, 44

Garibaldi, General Giuseppe 60, 66
gender
    church and 114–16
    family and 111, 114, 116; *see also* under hierarchism, hierarchies

genealogy
    biblical 5–6, 129
    databases 5, 36 (*see also* Ancestry.com)
genogram 120
Germany, Germans
    migrants 44
    Nazi 73
glossolalia see under speaking in tongues
Golden Rule, the 62–64
Gramsci, Antonio 70
Great Migration of Italians 21, 23, 43, 66, 68, 83, 84, 106
Greek philosophy 63

Handlin, Oscar 43
Harlem (NY) 81, 108
healing, divine 48, 92, 96–98
hierarchism, hierarchies
    the Catholic Church and 84
    gender and 114, 116
Hinduism 63
holistic health 123, 124, 126, 134
Holy Spirit 48, 49, 85, 92, 93, 95, 98, 116, 121; *see also* baptism, Spirit; Trinity, the

imago Dei 5, 75, 77, 114, 137
immigration: Act of 1965 44, 74; *see also* migration
individualism, individualistic 4, 35, 39, 80, 107, 122, 134, 136
Information Age 136
Ireland, Irish 1–2, 44, 84
Irish Americans 66–67
Islam, Muslim 63, 109
Italian Americans
    Catholicism and 80–81
    family and 108, 122
    Pentecostalism and 82–86
    race and 72 (*see also* Keltic vs. Iberic nomenclature)
    Sunday Dinner tradition and 11, 13–17, 60
Italian hymnal 46, 49
Italy, Italian
    emigration from 45–54

music culture and 130–31
    patriarchalism and 113
    Pentecostals and 13, 23, 46, 50, 78, 83–88, 91, 109, 115
    race and 36, 66–70, 73, 76
    social class and 59–62; *see also under* Catholic Church, Catholics, Catholicism

Jackson, Jesse 76
Japan, Japanese 44
Jefferson, Thomas 70, 71–72
Jerusalem Council 109
Jesus Christ 5–6, 48, 75, 87, 111, 129
Jews, Jewish 2, 18, 44, 63, 67, 73, 87, 94, 109
Jim Crow laws 68
John XXIII, Pope 87

"Keltic-Iberic" nomenclature
    northern Italian (Keltic) 67, 68
    southern Italian (Iberic) 67, 68–69, 72
Ketcham, Ralph 107
Kingdom of Italy 43, 60, 66–67, 91
King, Yolanda 65
Korea, Koreans 44

labels, ethnic or religious 1, 3, 73–74, 77, 129, 132
Latin America, Latin Americans 29, 31, 34–35, 70, 73
Latina/o 34, 73, 115
leadership
    in the church 113, 114
    servanthood and 116
Lee-Barnewall, Michelle 116
LGBTQ movement 115
Little Italies 22
Lord's Supper (Eucharist) 108
Loving v. Virginia (1967) 23
lynching
    of African Americans 69n17
    of Italians 69

Mafia 25, 73
mainline Christianity 79, 82, 85, 87, 92
Manji, Irshad 3

Margherita of Savoy, Queen 33
marriage
    children born out of wedlock 4, 101
    divorce and 4, 101
    intermarriage 21, 23
matriarchy, matriarchal 112, 113, 116
mealtimes, regular 108–9, 110, 135
Medina, Néstor 3
Mekonnen, Alemayehu 75
melting pot metaphor 2, 25, 135
mental health *see* mental illness; holistic health
mental illness
    anxiety and 35, 36, 95, 96, 117, 118, 120, 121, 122
    depression and 36, 95, 120n5
    psychiatric treatment and 118–19, 121, 132
    vicious cycle of worry and 118, 120, 125; *see also* holistic health
Methodists, Methodism 3, 86n21, 129–30
Mexico, Mexican 35, 73
Mezzogiorno 60, 104
migration
    emigration from Italy 21, 45, 47, 52, 53
    migrant identity 34, 43, 44, 54
    return 22, 106
    transatlantic passage and 21, 53, 61, 106, 108; *see also* Great Migration of Italians
Milan 47
Muhammad 63, 109
music and wellness 130–31, 135
Mussolini, Benito 87

Niagara Falls (NY) 48, 49, 81, 82
Naples, Neapolitan 33, 45
Napoleonic rule 51
nationalism, Italian 66–67
Native Americans (American Indians) 35–36, 44
nature (genetics) vs. nurture (environment) debate 121, 123–24
New York
    city 22–23, 46, 47, 50, 52, 72, 78
    harbor 53; state 49, 81
Noah 5–6, 129
North Avenue Mission 85
nuclear (*casa*) family 104–5, 106, 134

overprescribing 121

Paul, the apostle 28, 29, 81, 93, 96, 114, 116
Pentecostals, Pentecostalism 2, 11, 78, 80, 82, 84–88, 91–98, 113, 114–15, 122, 129–30; *see also under* Italy, Italian
performance mentality 120, 133–34
persecution 29, 81, 87, 88
Philippines 44
Piper, John 95
Pitrè, Giuseppe 53
Pius the IX, Pope 91
Plato 63
Poland, Poles 44, 83
politics, political
    in America 2, 107, 122
    in Italy 66, 72, 90
Portuguese 69
prayer
    corporate 14, 90, 93–94, 111–12, 113
    private 32, 89, 93–94, 131
    Second Vatican Council and 87
Presbyterian Church, Presbyterianism 46, 84, 86n21, 92
Prophecy 92, 96
Protestant, Protestantism 2, 79–80, 82, 84, 85, 87, 92
providence, divine 6, 97, 127–29
psychology, psychologists 120, 124, 134n2
Puerto Rico, Puerto Rican 34, 44, 73
Puglia 45, 59, 76

Qur'an 63

race issues
    America and 2, 36, 65, 67, 68, 69
    the interracial family 135–36
    North-South divide in Italy and 66
    racial blindness 73–75, 77

segregation 68; *see also* Black Codes; Jim Crow laws; slavery
Reconstruction era 68
Reformation, Protestant 86n22, 88
relational health 4, 121, 122, 124, 134
renewal, renewalist
    Charismatic 87, 91, 92; *see also* Pentecostal
riposa see siesta
Risorgimento (Italian unification) 33, 60
Rome
    ancient 81, 94
    1870 overthrow of 66–67
Russia, Russians 44

Sabbath (*Shabbath*) 11, 17–19, 109, 124, 130, 131, 135
Saggio, Joseph 35–36
Scandinavia, Scandinavian 25, 70
science
    evolutionary theory and 71, 128
    miracles and 96–97; *see also* social Darwinism
Scripture 6, 47, 63, 75, 85–86, 87, 88
Second Vatican Council (Vatican II) 85, 86–88; *see also under* prayer
secularity, secular 2, 98
segregation *see under* race issues
Sicily, Sicilian 22, 59, 66, 73, 105
siesta 26, 29–32, 124, 131–32, 135
slavery, slave trade 44, 68, 70
social class
    lower (peasant) 54, 60, 61
    middle 61, 66, 83
    upper 61, 66
social Darwinism 71, 72
social media 5, 136
Spain, Spanish 44, 60, 69, 70
Spanish flu 46
speaking in tongues
    glossolalia 93–95
    interpretation of 93
    xenolalia 93–94
spiritual (charismatic) gifts
    cessationism vs. *continuationism* 94
    ministry form of 92, 94
    miraculous form of 92
spirituality 79, 83, 86, 98

subsistent lifestyle 21, 50, 59, 104
supernatural, the 94, 96–98, 135; *see also* healing, divine
Sweden, Swedish, Swedes 44, 66, 67
Synan, Vinson 129
Syracuse (NY) 13, 15, 22–23, 37, 46, 81, 102

table fellowship 108–9
Taoism 63
theist, theistic, theism 4, 5, 97, 98, 126, 127–29
Thirteenth Amendment 68
Tolkien, J. R. R. 127
Tosetto, Massimiliano 45, 47–48, 82
Trinity, the 5, 76, 121

urban (industrial) America 22, 43, 66, 67, 92, 108
US Bill of Rights 122
US Bureau of the Census 84
US Bureau of Immigration 67
US Bureau of Labor Statistics 112

Vatican, the 66, 81, 91, 97; *see also* Second Vatican Council
Veneto 47
Victor Emmanuel II, reign of 51
Vietnam 44

watchmaker argument for God's existence 128
Wesley, John 129–30
Western society (culture) 4, 36, 80, 98, 101, 107, 134
World Wars: era 4; World War I (WWI) 46, 53; World War II (WWII) 107
worship 13, 19, 48, 49, 84–85, 87, 98, 110

xenolalia see under speaking in tongues

Yong, Amos 79–80

Zangwill, Israel 2
Zoroastrianism 63

Scripture Index

Genesis
Book of	6
1:26	5, 76
1:26–27	5
1:27	114
2	128
3	128
4	5
5	5
5:3	6
10	5
11	5
12:1–3	6

Exodus
20:8–10	18

Leviticus
19:18	63

Deuteronomy
32:7	33

1 Samuel
16:7	20

Psalms
100:5	126
103:17	1
127:2	27

Proverbs
1:8–9	101

Matthew
1	5
1:2–16	6
6:14	78
7:12	63

Mark
12:31	63n11

Luke
6:31	59, 63

Acts
Book of	92
2	93
2:6–11	93–94
15	109

Romans

8:28	29
12:2	117
12:6	92n3

1 Corinthians

Book of	93
12:10	93
12:31	92n3
14:3	96
14:5	93
14:13–15	93
14:28	93
14:34–35	114
16:20	13n18

2 Corinthians

Book of	28–29
12:10	28–29
13:12	13n18

Galatians

3:28	111, 114

Ephesians

4:12	116
5	114
5:21	114
5:22	114

Philippians

3:6	28

Colossians

3:23	29

1 Thessalonians

5:26	13n18

1 Peter

5:14	13

Revelation

5:9	135

www.ingramcontent.com/pod-product-compliance
Lightning Source LLC
Chambersburg PA
CBHW050806160426
43192CB00010B/1655